The United Methodist Primer

2005 Revised Edition

Chester E. Custer

An introduction to the journey of faith as traveled by United Methodists—and a survey of their history, beliefs, mission, and church organization.

DISCIPLESHIP RESOURCES

PO BOX 340003 • NASHVILLE, TN 37203-0003
www.discipleshipresources.org

Revised 2005

ISBN 0-88177-359-X

Library of Congress Catalog Card No. 2001091731

DR359

CONTENTS

ACKNOWLEDGEMENTS

To put into one short book all that needs to be said about the history, beliefs, and mission of The United Methodist Church seemed to be an overwhelming task. Our libraries are filled with material by authors who have researched all of these areas, and more. It became immediately apparent to me that all I could hope to do in a primer was to give a brief overview of the most important aspects of the subject. In selecting what should be included, undoubtedly important subjects were omitted. In light of this, I invite you as a reader to explore further what I have only touched on.

Many people over the years have helped me on this assignment. Indeed, as I ponder my indebtedness to others, I recall my own Christian pilgrimage. I recall those who helped me as a young student pastor in The United Brethren Church, as a seminary student in The Evangelical United Brethren Church, as a pastor in The Methodist Church, and then later as a staff member of the General Board of Discipleship of The United Methodist Church. Writing about these several denominations took me back over some familiar territory.

I was first approached to write *The United Methodist Primer* by my colleagues in Discipleship Resources. Ezra Earl Jones, who was General Secretary of the General Board of Discipleship, and Noé Gonzales encouraged me to do it. Thus, the task began.

I am especially indebted to my wife, Elizabeth, with whom I discussed the subject areas covered in the text, and who read and critiqued the manuscript from its inception to its completion. The contributions she made to the content are apparent to me throughout the book.

George Koehler was most helpful in offering counsel. I am also indebted to others who reviewed the first draft. Duane Ewers, Neil

Alexander, Nellie Moser, Noé Gonzales, Frank Gulley, and Bishop George Bashore all gave me suggestions and correctives that have improved the text.

It is my hope and prayer that you may find within the words written a clearer word that will help you on your Christian pilgrimage.

CHESTER E. CUSTER

CHAPTER ONE

OUR JOURNEY OF FAITH

e are all beginners in the Christian faith. We are a pilgrim people taking up our journey anew each day, walking into the unknown, trusting in God. Indeed, that is the story of the church. It is the story of a searching God and a seeking people. It is the Emmaus story of the risen Christ, who joins us on our journey and walks with us (Luke 24:13-35). It is your story and mine. Thus, as we try to understand the nature and mission of The United Methodist Church, we begin with our journey of faith.

What has been the story of your faith journey? Are you just beginning? Have you been a long time on the road? Are you a discouraged traveler? Have you been captured by a new vision? What does a profile of your pilgrimage look like? Mine has its new beginnings, its peaks and valleys, its wanderings and plateaus. I doubt if anyone's spiritual journey is always an onward and upward ascent.

We are continually en route, continually in the process of becoming, always in the midst of change. We know both victory and defeat. We have to cope with agonizing problems and shattering experiences. We never reach the place on our Christian pilgrimage where there are no more problems to contend with, or when we can say, "Now I have arrived." We walk by faith and live by trust, greeting the challenge of each new day. At least this is true of most of us as disciples of Jesus Christ.

We have been given no assurance that faith in God will spare us disappointment, trouble, or sorrow. Not at all. Some of the most faithful people I know have experienced great tragedy, failure, and disappointment. We face many of the same problems and temptations others do. In fact, we are likely to become even more sensitive to human need and to problems of which others may be unaware or do not heed. But we can face each day and every circumstance with the assurance that God is with us in the good and the bad, in success and failure, in life and death. We are not alone. That is indeed good news.

This is the gospel we affirm as United Methodists. It assures us that God's grace—God's unmerited love—surrounds us and encourages us, goes before us and upholds us. This gospel envisions a new creation, "a new heaven and a new earth" (Revelation 21:1). It looks forward to a day when this world will be transformed by the spirit of the Eternal. We are even invited to help bring that day nearer. Our faith is grounded in this kind of vision.

The Assurance of Things Hoped For

How would you define faith? It's hard to answer that question in a few words. Faith has as many facets as a fine-cut diamond. The author of the Book of Hebrews defines faith as "the assurance of things hoped for, the conviction of things not seen" (Hebrews 11:1). In a discussion of the nature of Christian faith, members of one adult Sunday school class talked about these three perspectives:

1. *Faith is what we believe*—the creed or concepts we hold—as well as *how we live*. It is with this latter understanding of faith—the faith that helps us to live with a spirit of hope, to trust, to begin again once we have failed—that we are now concerned.

2. *Faith means centering our life in God and on the will of God*. It is keeping our life open to God's leading and to the presence of the Holy Spirit. Faith involves a daily walk with Jesus Christ. Faith means putting our ultimate, not our conditional, trust in God. Faith is trusting that God will help us reach that state of obedience that was modeled for us in Jesus Christ.

3. *Faith is both a gift and a response*. It is a gift in the sense that God's love is freely given to each of us (1 John 4:7-19). Faith is also a response, in that we can choose (or not) to live in terms of that love revealed in Christ.

The statements that follow are ways some have tried to explain the implications of faith. You will have your own examples of what faith means to you.

- Faith is living in terms of hope and making our decisions on the basis of hope. Faith gives us a vision of what can be. It is seeing the best in the worst of conditions. Faith gives a person the benefit of the doubt. It turns negatives into positives, despair into promise. Faith is redemptive and transforming.
- Faith is deciding, in spite of our limitations, to assume responsibilities that seem impossible for us and to do the best we can. Faith is seeking to go where we believe God is calling us to go and to do what we believe God is calling us to do.
- Faith lends heart and hands to lift up those who are fallen. Faith identifies with the poor, the hungry, the oppressed—those with whom Christ suffers. It does not shrink from the magnitude of a problem. Faith never gives up.
- Faith is trusting God to sustain and direct us in the choices and changes related to our daily work as we take on a new job, lose a job, or retire. In all of these transitions, we learn to take one step at a time, one day at a time, believing that, as we walk, a path will open before us.
- Faith is knowing that God stands with us in the hour of separation, abandonment, or death. We are assured that our agony and pain are matched by healing love and grace. Faith is the parent saying after the death of a child, "Underneath are the everlasting arms."

Beginning Where We Are

We always begin the journey of faith where we are, just as we are. God accepts us on these terms. One need not have achieved some stage of excellence before making a beginning. We come to God in faith because our souls hunger and thirst for the Eternal. We come because we need God. And we continue in pilgrimage because we have discovered that our deepest yearnings and highest hopes are matched by the grace of God revealed in Christ.

Jesus said that if we have faith the size of a mustard seed, we can move mountains (Matthew 17:20). That is, faith in God makes it possible to do seemingly impossible things. Faith removes obstacles that seem insurmountable; faith transforms problems into opportunities. Faith may involve us in personal relationships and commitments that are far from firm and secure. Faith dares to risk and fail, if need be. It dares to go on trusting even in the midst of impending defeat.

Our faith may be shaken at times. Jesus himself seems to have experienced this. When Jesus needed them most, Peter, a trusted disciple, denied him, and Judas betrayed him. And as Jesus faced the cross, he cried out to God, "Why have you forsaken me?" (Matthew 27:46). Such times can come to us not because we lack faith, or because we have been unfaithful, but because we have followed the course of obedience. On the other hand, we have all known times when our faith has grown weak and has wavered because of disobedience. We have not kept our heart fixed on the One whose ways are above our ways. And we cry out, "O God, forgive me and be merciful to me. Use the errors of my way that I may become a new person."

God Is Faithful

In all the ups and downs of faith, the plateaus and deep valleys, God is faithful. Time and again the Bible assures us that God does not forsake us.

- "The LORD is faithful...and gracious... The LORD upholds all who are falling, and raises up all who are bowed down" (Psalm 145:13-14).
- "It is the LORD your God who goes with you; [God] will not fail you or forsake you" (Deuteronomy 31:6).
- "The LORD is my shepherd, I shall not want.... Even though I walk through the darkest valley, I fear no evil; for you are with me" (Psalm 23:1, 4).
- "Let us hold fast to the confession of our hope without wavering, for [God] who has promised is faithful" (Hebrews 10:23).

Though we stumble and fall, God is with us. Though we turn against God, God does not turn against us. Though we go astray and lose our way, there is One who searches for us (Matthew 18:12-14). Matthew records the birth of Jesus with the most wonderful words in Scripture: "'They shall name him Emmanuel,' which means, 'God is with us'" (Matthew 1:23). It is no wonder that we lift our voices, "O for a thousand tongues to sing my great Redeemer's praise!"[1] What a gospel we claim that God is with us on our journey and will not forsake us.

A New Relationship Through Faith

John Wesley believed that faith is the foundation for everything else. He understood faith as a vital trust in God—as our grateful acceptance of God's gift of pardon, as the assurance that our lives have come under the merciful and healing love of Christ. Wesley confirmed the apostle Paul's conviction that we have all sinned and fallen short of the glory of God, and that we are justified by God's grace through faith (Romans 3:23-24, 28). We share these convictions as United Methodists.

Faith initiates us into a new relationship with God. God's unlimited love helps us face up to our lives and know that forgiveness comes with repentance. It is knowing that Christ breaks "the power of cancelled sin" and sets us free.[2] Grace triumphs in our lives. We are no longer alienated from God. We can return home, knowing that the door will be open. That is what it means to be justified: We are pilgrims assured of God's sufficient grace. Think about how faith in God has changed your attitudes and shaped your values, how faith has helped you to be a new person in Christ.

The Church as a Pilgrim People

The Christian's pilgrimage of faith is never simply an individual undertaking. We are part of a great company of the faithful on a journey together. We encourage and support one another. As our own spiritual journey connects with the spiritual pilgrimages of others, a sense of community emerges. Together we share not only our challenges and failures but also our experiences of God's powerful grace creating new life out of our experiences together.

The Scripture affirms the importance of each person's spiritual pilgrimage. But the Bible also has much to say about the community of faith. The Old Testament tells about a people walking together with God, who is their cloud by day and fire by night (Exodus 13:22). Hans Küng reminds us:

> The Church is always and everywhere a living people, gathered together from the peoples of this world and journeying through the midst of time. The Church is essentially *en route*, on a journey, a pilgrimage. A Church which pitches its tents without looking out constantly for new horizons, which does not continually strike camp, is being untrue to its calling. The historical nature of the Church is revealed by the fact that it remains a pilgrim people of God.[3]

To be "a pilgrim people of God" reflects a New Testament under-standing of Jesus, who is called the "pioneer and perfecter of our faith" (Hebrews 12:2). A pioneer is one who blazes new trails, goes before us, travels lightly, breaks camp, and moves on. The pioneer knows that obstacles will be encountered, new paths will need to be cleared, and risks taken. But that is what faith is all about for pilgrim people, both as the church and as individual Christian disciples.

Faith in Action

Living by faith means venturing out and, therefore, moving ahead with the vision before us. It involves commitment to the things we believe Christ is concerned about. It means giving hands and feet to what our heart affirms. Wesley believed that faith is not simply "a train of ideas in the head"; it is also "a disposition of the heart."[4] It involves the will. What we believe and how we express our belief are both important; they interact with each other and belong together. The Letter of James points out the ineffectiveness of faith without works:

> If a brother or sister is naked and lacks daily food, and one of you says to them, "Go in peace; keep warm and eat your fill," and yet you do not supply their bodily needs, what is the good of that? So faith by itself, if it has no works, is dead.
> (James 2:15-17)

We may give assent to all the creeds of the church, but they can amount to little if they fail to express themselves in our daily lives. Faith involves commitment expressed in action, trust, and obedience.

Faith, therefore, includes both an inward and an outward journey. We all know people who are always present when there is a Bible study or a worship service. The expression of their inward spiritual journey is important and meaningful. We also know people we can always count on to help with the projects for feeding the hungry, providing for the needs of the poor, or taking a stand on social issues. Their expression of their outward journey is also important and meaningful. But how many people do we know who fully express both an inward journey and an outward journey? With a committed faith, an inward journey of prayer, Bible study, and spiritual formation must run parallel to our outward journey of ministry and service. Traveled together, though, these two journeys lead us toward wholeness.

God's Intended Purpose

Faith leads us to seek God's will for our own lives, as well as for the church, our community, and the world. What is God's intended purpose? Where does the journey eventually lead? Toward what end?

Jesus identified that end as the rule or reign of God. He spoke of it as the kingdom of God, or the kingdom of heaven. (These were terms he used interchangeably.) The Kingdom signifies God's will and rule within our lives, in our world, and in the fuller life beyond death. We, as individual Christians and as the church, are called to live in terms of God's promised kingdom. Jesus spoke of the Kingdom as being within us. He also implied that the Kingdom is among us and beyond us. Being a part of the Kingdom means living within the presence and under the loving care of the Eternal. It means living in terms of "thy will be done on earth as it is in heaven."[5]

The nature of faith leads us toward the coming day of *shalom*, that day when compassion, justice, righteousness, and peace shall be the inheritance of all the peoples of the earth. It will be a day when "the wolf shall live with the lamb" (Isaiah 11:6), when swords shall be beaten into plowshares and "nation shall not lift up sword against nation" (Isaiah 2:4), and when the Christmas story of peace on earth becomes a reality (Luke 2:14). It will be a day when the starving people of the earth will hunger and thirst no more and refugees will have a home. Yes, this hope is a vision of the world as we believe God intends it to be. It is just such a dream that has inspired the people of faith through the centuries.

The reality of an alienated and broken world calls us to a ministry of reconciliation. The reality of people who are hurting and in need of love and support calls us to a ministry of compassion. Each of us can begin with ourself, in our own home and community, by reaching out to someone in need, to someone carrying a heavy burden. Individually, and as a congregation, we can seek ways to address the issues of peace and justice, human dignity, poverty, hunger. You will find no difficulty in extending this list of human needs.

Even though there are multitudes of problems that cry out to us, wherein we believe God's purpose is yet to be realized, there are also signs of God's presence and purpose now being fulfilled in our midst. In that sense, the Kingdom is here among us. The Kingdom is here; it is yet to be. It is a present reality; it is a future hope. We have a glimpse of what God's ultimate purpose is for all creation in Jesus Christ. In what ways do you see God's purpose for your life, and for our world, as a present reality?

The author of Hebrews recalls the lives of the faithful on their journey of faith: "All of these died in faith without having received the promises," but they saw it and greeted it from afar. They sought a homeland, a better country, a heavenly one that God had prepared for them (Hebrews 11:13-16). The Promised Land toward which their pilgrimage was leading them in this life became a reality in a fuller sense as they crossed over the last divide. We, too, may die in the faith without having entered into the fullness of God's intended kingdom; yet, we hail it from afar.

John Wesley's final words are said to have been, "The best of all is, God is with us." God does not abandon us at death. God will complete the journey of faith with us and uphold us on our final crossing. Earth's journey will then be complete, but the heavenly pilgrimage only begun.

What a gospel we claim for our lives and for our world. What a message the church has to proclaim. What a challenge to begin living and acting here and now as those who are captured by a vision from on high. That is the faith we affirm and aspire to as United Methodists.

> We are not alone, we live in God's world.
> We believe in God:
>   who has created and is creating,
>   who has come in Jesus, the Word made flesh,
>   to reconcile and make new,
>   who works in us and others by the Spirit.
> We trust in God.
> We are called to be the church:
>   to celebrate God's presence,
>   to love and serve others,
>   to seek justice and resist evil,
>   to proclaim Jesus, crucified and risen,
>   our judge and our hope.
> In life, in death, in life beyond death,
>   God is with us.
> We are not alone.
> Thanks be to God. Amen.[6]

CHAPTER TWO

UNITED IN CHRIST

What does it mean to be a United Methodist Christian? How would you respond to a friend who asked you that question? We United Methodists are a pilgrim people on a journey of faith under the lordship of Jesus Christ. Yet, we are part of a much larger community of faith, one that encircles the globe and spans the centuries. A multitude of faithful people have gone before us and have helped bring us to where we are now on our spiritual journey. We have drawn strength and inspiration from the lives of many of them. Think of the people who have been important on your own spiritual journey. Who were they? What was it about them that has given you encouragement?

Together with other Christians we seek to be attentive to the voice of the Spirit and obedient to the One who leads us. Our very name— The United Methodist Church—is a strong reminder of who we are and what we are called to be. We will be considering throughout this book what it means to be the *church*, and in particular what the characteristics are of The United *Methodist* Church. Let us consider here what it means to be *united*.

How Are We United?

The word *United* in our denominational name is part of our church tradition and has historical roots. In 1946, the Church of the United Brethren in Christ and The Evangelical Church came together to form The Evangelical United Brethren Church. And in 1968, The Evangelical United Brethren Church merged with The Methodist

Church to form what we now know as The United Methodist Church. So, the *United* in our church name has been not only a term preserved through these mergers, but it also represents the actual uniting of these different denominations.

We are also united through a connectional system of church government whereby each congregation is united with all others throughout the entire denomination. The connectional system that coordinates and links together the work and ministry of the church goes back to our denominational founders. The early societies and congregations that came into being as a result of the work of Wesley and Asbury, Otterbein and Boehm, and Albright were connected through an itinerant ministry and by conferences.

But that is not the end of the story. We are united in other ways as well. We are united with Christ. We are united in and through Christ with a great company of other Christians at home and around the world. We are united as a servant people to all those for whom Christ died. And we are united with those "who have finished their course in faith."[1]

United With Christ

Most important, we seek to be united with Christ. That is the Christian's heartbeat, the life of the church. Union with Christ is primary for us as United Methodists, as well as for all who claim the name of Christian. We accept and proclaim Jesus as the long-awaited Messiah, our Savior and the Savior of the world. We confess with Peter that Jesus is "the Messiah" (Matthew 16:16). We affirm with the apostle Paul that God's love is revealed in Christ, who died for us (Romans 5:8). We proclaim the message of the Fourth Gospel, that the "Word became flesh and lived among us..., full of grace and truth" (John 1:14). That is why being united with Christ is so important. The analogy of the vine and the branches that Jesus gave describes this relationship:

> Abide in me as I abide in you. Just as the branch cannot bear
> fruit by itself unless it abides in the vine, neither can you unless
> you abide in me. I am the vine, you are the branches.
> (John 15:4-5)

Abiding in Christ means opening the door of the heart and inviting Christ into our lives. It is letting Christ take charge of our lives and praying that Christ's spirit will be formed in us by faith. It is seeking to have the mind and spirit of Christ in all that we do.

The apostle Paul writes that we are baptized into Christ (Romans 6:3). That is to say, we are baptized into the fellowship that exists through Jesus Christ and are baptized into a relationship wherein Christ's presence encourages and sustains us on life's pilgrimage. Baptism symbolizes the self-giving love and gracious acceptance of God revealed in Christ. To be "in Christ" through faith and baptism is to share in a new quality of life that Christ brings.

Paul also says that whoever is in Christ is a "new creation" (2 Corinthians 5:17). The old has passed away; the new has come. Our lives are transformed by Christ's presence and by the Holy Spirit working within us. When Christ's spirit lives within us, when we are united with Christ, all things become new.

Those who are truly in Christ do not presume to be superior to others or withdraw to themselves. Nor do they assume they have an inside track on the spiritual journey. They do not exemplify a holier-than-thou attitude. Quite the contrary: They hunger and thirst after righteousness; they are humble before God and others; they strive to be merciful and pure in heart; they are peacemakers.

To be united with Christ is to share the vision of which Jesus spoke in the Sermon on the Mount, a vision of life claimed by God. It is a vision partly within our grasp, yet always beyond our full realization. If there is any one thing you and I, and the church, should pray for and strive for, it is to be united with Christ and in Christ. From that spiritual relationship everything else flows.

United Through Christ With Others

As we learn more about what it means to be a new creation in Christ, we become more aware of what it means to live in Christian community. We are united through Christ with others. That is how the church began. The church came into being as a fellowship of people committed to Jesus Christ. The New Testament calls it the *koinonia*: the fellowship of believers who celebrated Christ's presence among them, who cared deeply for one another, and who served others in the name of Christ. The litany celebrating our church union in 1968 emphasized that we are united in and through Christ.

We are united with others in faith and outreach in our own congregations. To be united through Christ with others provides a bond of fellowship. The fellowship becomes our spiritual family. We share one hope, "one Lord, one faith, one baptism" (Ephesians 4:5). This does not mean that we will all agree on everything. But the love of Christ we seek to make central in our lives is broad enough to help us use different points of view as learning experiences and for the mutual upbuilding of us all. Within my own congregation I find people who genuinely care about others, who are understanding and supportive. Their lives have come under the discipline of Christ. We are united through Christ with one another and for others. What are some ways in which your congregation is that kind of Christian fellowship?

After having experienced God's grace in his life, Jacob Albright, founder of The Evangelical Church, said that one should "be ready at all times to fight the good fight of faith...in fellowship with devout Christians, and to take part in bearing the cross, to pray for and with one another, to be vigilant and edify each other...in the service of God."[2] That is at the heart of Christian witness and evangelism.

The Christian fellowship, of course, includes more than members of our own congregation. We are united with brothers and sisters in Christ from other churches as well—within and beyond The United Methodist Church. We are united with Christians who likely will not see things just as we do. John Wesley said, "Though we cannot think alike, may we not love alike? May we not be of one heart, though we are not of one opinion?"[3] We believe there is no one person, no one church, that has all the truth. Rather, we are all seeking a fuller understanding of God's will and a clearer vision of how to express it in our world today. We need one another.

A Cloud of Witnesses

We are also united with those who have finished their course in faith. The author of Hebrews refers to them as "a cloud of witnesses" (Hebrews 12:1). They, too, are part of our spiritual family. In one version of the service for the celebration of the Lord's Supper, we pray these words: "We remember with thanksgiving those who have loved and served thee in thy Church on earth, who now rest from their labors."[4]

We are united with multitudes of Christians we have never known by name, as well as with those who are familiar to us: Mother Teresa of Calcutta, who bound up the wounds of the leper and cradled the hungry and dying in her arms; Martin Luther King, Jr., slain civil rights leader, who was an exponent of justice and freedom from oppression; John R. Mott, an ecumenical pioneer and champion of young people who declared the urgency of bringing the world to Christ; Dietrich Bonhoeffer, martyred by the Nazis, whose letters and theological writings still influence Christian thought today. These and many others are part of our spiritual family.

Back Through History

Our United Methodist heritage goes back to John and Charles Wesley and Francis Asbury, to Martin Boehm and Philip William Otterbein, and to Jacob Albright, about whom we will have more to say later.

Martin Luther, who spearheaded the Protestant Reformation; John Hus, who was burned at the stake because he refused to recant what he believed was God's revealed will for his life and the church; John Wyclif, who was instrumental in translating the Bible into English and who spoke out about the need for church reform—they, too, are our ancestors in the faith.

Every time we pray, "Lord, make me an instrument of your peace," we confess that we are one with Saint Francis of Assisi, who renounced a life of wealth to care for the poor. When we acknowledge our need to make prayer more a part of our lives, when we long for humility and simplicity, we know that Saint Teresa of Avila speaks for us. When we remember who we are, and Who it is that calls us, we confess with Augustine:

> Narrow is the mansion of my soul; enlarge Thou it, that Thou mayest enter in. It is ruinous; repair Thou it.... Lord, cleanse me from my secret faults, and spare Thy servant from the power of the enemy.[5]

Back to the New Testament

Our roots go back, of course, to Jesus, the Promised One of God, the Messiah, the Christ, the One who is the pivotal point of our faith, the head of the church. Millions have found in Christ the One who is truly human and truly divine, their Redeemer, and the Savior of the world. We have seen God's purpose and love perfectly revealed in the life, death, and resurrection of Jesus Christ. That is why we sing, "Lord, I want to be a Christian."[6]

Our roots go back to Mary and Joseph, who brought Jesus up in the Jewish faith; to his brothers and sisters, who did not understand him. We are united in faith with the twelve whom Jesus chose as disciples: Simon Peter, who, in spite of his denial, became "a rock" in the early church; James and John, who left their nets to follow the Galilean; doubting Thomas; and Matthew the tax collector. Mary Magdalene, who announced the Resurrection, and the family of Mary, Martha, and Lazarus—they, too, belong to our United Methodist heritage. Lydia, a follower of the Way; Timothy and Barnabas, missionaries along with Paul, whose letters are our earliest New Testament records; and the authors of our Gospels—they are all our brothers and sisters in the faith.

And Back to the Old Testament

Our spiritual lineage does not begin with the New Testament. Nailed to the cross of Jesus was the inscription "This is the King of the Jews" (Luke 23:38). Most of Jesus' first disciples were Jews, who claimed a long Hebrew tradition. The early Christians saw in the Old Testament that which prepared the way for the coming of the Messiah. But they also knew that they were part of the covenant people of God. They were a people under a new covenant, called by God, united with Christ and with one another.

So it is that we are united through Christ with prophets such as Micah, who said that what the Lord requires is "to do justice, and to love kindness, and to walk humbly" with God (Micah 6:8), and Isaiah, who looked forward to the coming of the One who would be called "Wonderful Counselor, Mighty God, Everlasting Father, Prince of Peace" (Isaiah 9:6); and to a day when nations would not "lift up sword against nation" (Isaiah 2:4).

We are united on our pilgrimage with Naomi and with Ruth, who cried out, "Your people shall be my people, and your God my God" (Ruth 1:16). And with the psalmist who sang, "My help comes from the LORD, who made heaven and earth" (Psalm 121:2). And with Moses, who led the Israelites out of bondage and who received the

Commandments. Our lineage goes back to Sarah and to Abraham, who went out in faith "not knowing where he was going" (Hebrews 11:8).

What's in a name? What does it mean to be united? It means that we never walk alone. Multitudes of pilgrims, captured by a vision of the Eternal, have gone on before us. In all their struggles to be faithful to God's faithfulness, God's covenant has been their bond. God's faithfulness has been a covenant that has united them with God and one another. We are part of that "endless line of splendor."[7]

Into the World About Us

It is also well for us to remember that we are called to be present with those in the world about us, those who may not share our religious convictions and who may never be seen inside a church. Like our Lord, we are to take upon ourselves their pain and loneliness and to help them bear their burdens. We are united through Christ with them, too, because Christ suffers with those who reach out for life and hope. Often, the journey of faith takes us through the territory of the estranged, the neglected, the lonely and oppressed. Think of someone to whom you might go, or ought to go, someone you can help on your Christian journey.

Toyohiko Kagawa, who worked among the slums of Japan, revealed the spirit of the One who lived for others:

> Oh, my soul! My soul! Do you hear God's pain-pitched cry as
> He suffers because of the world's sore distress? God dwells
> among the lowliest of [people]. He sits on the dust heap among
> the prison convicts. With the juvenile delinquents He stands at
> the door, begging bread. He throngs with the beggars at the
> place of alms. He is among the sick. He stands in line with the
> unemployed. Therefore, let [those of us] who would meet God
> visit the prison cell before going to the temple. Before [we] go
> to church let [us] visit the hospital. Before [we] read the Bible
> let [us] help the beggar standing at [our] door![8]

The Gospel of Matthew depicts the Last Judgment as a time when the blessed shall hear, "Just as you did it to one of the least of these…you did it to me" (Matthew 25:40).

Yes, we are united with Christ. We are united in and through Christ with a multitude of the faithful near at home, around the world, and across the centuries. We are united with those for whom Christ died and with whom Christ now suffers. We are united as a church. That is the faith we affirm. That is the vision to which we seek to be faithful. To be united in Christ, to be a pilgrim people, the people of the cross and flame, is indeed a high calling. We pray for grace and strength to claim it for ourselves and for our church.

CHAPTER THREE

OUR METHODIST
ROOTS

he streams of spiritual life that came
together to form The United Methodist
Church had their origins in the evangelistic
outreach and ministries of John and
Charles Wesley and Francis Asbury
(Methodist Church), Philip William Otterbein and Martin Boehm
(United Brethren Church), and Jacob Albright (Evangelical Church).
All were claimed by a common faith and zeal. Each of them emphasized
the authority of the Scripture, a personal spiritual experience of salvation
through faith in Christ, and love expressed in service to others.

The churches that came together to form The United Methodist
Church in 1968 held the same fundamental doctrines of faith, tracing their
theological traditions to the Protestant Reformation and to Wesleyanism.
They had similar ecclesiastical structures and an almost two-hundred-year
history of relationship.

Each of them was influenced by the pietistic emphasis on the spiritual
life. The Methodist Church had its beginning in the Church of England,
whereas The United Brethren Church and The Evangelical Church had
their origin in the spiritual awakening that occurred in America in the
late eighteenth and early nineteenth centuries. We will look at these
churches separately and try to capture something of our heritage.

In this chapter, we will survey our Methodist origins in the England
of the Wesleys and on the American frontier. In Chapters Four and
Five, we will turn to our Evangelical United Brethren origins in Germany
and America—the United Brethren branch in Chapter Four and the

23

Evangelical branch in Chapter Five. Then, in Chapter Six, we will pick up the story of all these denominations in the nineteenth and twentieth centuries.

The Wesleys

We begin in the little community of Epworth, England, the town where the founder of Methodism was born. It was there that the Wesleys lived. Samuel Wesley was the pastor of St. Andrew's Church, a parish church of the Church of England. The little stone church where he preached still stands on the edge of the village, and he is buried outside in the churchyard. John Wesley was born in Epworth on June 17, 1703.

On February 9, 1709, a fire swept through the parsonage. The family ran outside to safety. One child after another was accounted for, but five-year-old John was missing. The profile of John standing at an upstairs window inside the burning building could be seen. Samuel rushed back into the house to rescue John, but the flames pushed Samuel back. Then, one neighbor stood on the shoulders of another, and John jumped safely into the man's arms. Susanna, John's mother, regarded John's rescue as providential. Later she wrote that he was "a brand plucked out of the burning." She believed that her son had been saved for a special destiny. It was something John never forgot.

It has been recorded that Samuel and Susanna had as many as nineteen children, but only ten survived to adulthood. Susanna, in particular, had a profound influence on the children, as she was their spiritual mentor and school teacher. She set aside one hour a week for each child's spiritual instruction and nurture. John's hour was after the evening meal on Thursday. He was so impressed with this practice that, years later as a university student, he wrote to his mother asking her to still keep that hour for him—an hour that "would be as useful now for correcting my heart as it was then for forming my judgment."[1]

To School and to Georgia

By the time John was eleven, he could read English, Latin, and Greek. He left his home in Epworth with a scholarship to attend Charterhouse School in London more than 150 miles away. He remained there until he was seventeen, when he entered Christ Church College, Oxford University, on another scholarship. His father, grandfather, and great grandfather Wesley had all studied at Oxford, as had his grandfather Annesley, his mother's father, who was a popular non-Conformist preacher. John's older brother, Samuel, Jr., and his younger brother, Charles, were also Oxford graduates.

John never forgot his mother's conviction that his life had been spared for a special purpose. He was becoming more and more convinced that God was calling him into the ministry.

During Charles Wesley's Oxford days, he became part of a group of students that met on a regular basis in order to encourage one another in the faith. By this time, John had completed his work at the university and had gone to be a curate (assistant) in his father's church. Returning to Oxford later, he began to meet with the students and soon became their leader. In addition to practicing the spiritual disciplines of Bible study, prayer, and fasting, the group regularly visited the prison, taught the children of the poor, and visited the sick.

The group was both praised and criticized. They were ridiculed as "Bible Moths" and as the "Holy Club." Because of the highly disciplined, methodical way they lived, they were also nicknamed "Methodists." It was a name that stuck.

Within six months after their father died, John and Charles were on their way to Georgia with General James Edward Oglethorpe. Oglethorpe invited John to become a pastor to the settlers in Georgia, and John accepted with dreams of being a missionary to the Indians. Charles was chosen to go along as Oglethorpe's secretary. They set sail for America in October 1735.

John frankly confessed that one reason for going to Georgia was to save his own soul. On board ship he was impressed by the strong faith and simple trust of a group of Moravians. They were confident and calm when storms rocked the small ship. While in Georgia, a Moravian pastor, Augustus Spangenberg, asked John, "Do you know Jesus Christ?" Wesley replied, "I know he is the Saviour of the world." "True, but do you know he has saved you?" John replied in the affirmative, but later wrote in his journal, "I fear they were vain words."[2] Even though the missionary undertaking in itself was considered a failure by both John and Charles, it was the prelude to a great turning point in the lives of both brothers.

Spiritual Awakening

Charles returned to London in 1736, and John a year and a half later. While in London, they met Peter Böhler, a young Moravian who was about to leave for America. When John's spirit was so low that he wondered if he could even continue preaching, it was Böhler who told him to "preach faith till you have it; and then, *because* you have it, you *will* preach faith."[3]

Shortly thereafter, Charles, suffering from pleurisy, was taken to the home of John Bray, whom Charles said later was "a poor ignorant mechanic, who knows nothing but Christ."[4] It was there that a friend read Luther's remarks on the second chapter of Galatians: "He loved me and gave himself for me." There, too, Bray's sister said, "In the name of Jesus of Nazareth, arise, and believe, and thou shalt be healed of all thy infirmities."[5]

Charles took the words as a message from God and said, "I now found myself at peace with God, and rejoiced in hope of loving Christ."[6] Two days later, on May 23, 1738, Charles said, "I began a hymn upon my conversion."[7] That hymn might be called the birth song of the Methodist Revival.

> Where shall my wondering soul begin?
> How shall I all to heaven aspire?
> A slave redeemed from death and sin,
> A brand plucked from eternal fire…[8]

The next day, May 24, 1738, John Wesley wrote in his journal:

> In the afternoon I was asked to go to St. Paul's [Cathedral].
> The anthem was, "Out of the deep have I called unto thee, O
> Lord"… In the evening I went very unwillingly to a society in
> Aldersgate-Street, where one was reading Luther's preface to
> the Epistle to the Romans. About a quarter before nine, while
> he was describing the change which God works in the heart
> through faith in Christ, I felt my heart strangely warmed. I felt
> I did trust in Christ, Christ alone for salvation: And an assur-
> ance was given me, that he had taken away *my* sins, even *mine,*
> and saved *me* from the law of sin and death.[9]

John and his friends rushed to Charles' sick room, and John cried out, "I believe!" They sang together the hymn Charles had penned the morning before. The Wesleyan Revival had begun, and from that point on, the lives of both John and Charles Wesley took on a new vitality. Three weeks after his Aldersgate experience, John journeyed to Herrnhut, a small village in what is now East Germany. A strong Moravian settlement there was led by Count Zinzendorf. John was still very much aware of the influence of the Moravian friends he had met in Georgia, as well as that of Peter Böhler. His trip to Herrnhut would confirm the victory of faith climaxed by his heartwarming experience. He hoped "those holy men [at Herrnhut] who were themselves living witnesses of the full power of faith"[10] would establish his soul.

John returned to England shortly thereafter and never tired of preaching about God's gift of forgiving love, freely given to all, and of the assurance that comes through faith in Christ. A newfound joy and enthusiasm had come into his life. It was good news that he had to tell everyone, including those who never set foot inside a church.

A Revival Begins

Wesley's friend George Whitefield, who had been a member of the Holy Club at Oxford and who was about to leave for America, had been attracting great throngs of spiritually neglected people in England through his field preaching. Wesley himself thought this kind of preaching would be out of character for him. Yet, when Wesley preached to a crowd of about three thousand from an open field on April 2, 1739, he knew that a new phase of his life's work had begun.

Eventually, he preached in the open air all over England to miners and humble townspeople, barmaids and farmers, industrial workers, and anyone who would listen.

One of the best-known episodes of John Wesley's career occurred in Epworth, where he was born. When he returned to Epworth in 1742, seven years after his father's death, he found that his home church, where his father had preached for thirty-nine years, where he had been baptized and had served as curate, was closed to him. The pastor would not permit this field preacher, who held church outdoors and attracted enthusiastic crowds, to preach from his pulpit. One of Wesley's friends told the people leaving the Sunday service that John would preach there at six o'clock in the evening.

Wesley recorded in his journal: "Accordingly at six I came, and found such a congregation as I believe Epworth never saw before. I stood...upon my father's tombstone, and cried, 'The kingdom of heaven is not meat and drink; but righteousness, and peace, and joy in the Holy Ghost.' "[11] Whether from an open field, along the street, in a mine pit, or from a graveyard, Wesley seized every opportunity to proclaim the gospel of Christ.

The revival continued to spread, and thousands of people who came to hear John Wesley were converted under his preaching. Opposition to his ministry outside the established church only served to intensify the zeal of those who had found new life in Christ. It soon became apparent that some kind of organization was needed to bring the people together on a regular basis so that they could be sustained and nurtured in the faith. Therefore, societies were soon formed.

The rapid growth of the societies required more preachers and a closer organization. Wesley chose lay preachers and set them apart to do the full work of ministry, except administering the sacraments. Soon the societies became so large that it was necessary to divide them into classes of about a dozen people. These classes met weekly and were guided by a lay class leader.

Methodism Spreads to America

The Wesleyan Revival soon extended beyond England into Ireland, Scotland, and Wales. It spread to America. The words of Wesley "I look upon all the world as my parish"[12] were becoming a reality.

A number of men and women whose lives had been touched by the Wesleyan Revival came to America and began to bear witness to their faith in Christ. Among them were Robert and Elizabeth Strawbridge, Philip and Margaret Embury, Paul and Barbara Heck, Captain Thomas Webb, Richard Boardman, and Joseph Pilmore. Later on, in 1771, Francis Asbury, who had received little formal education but had been converted when he was about fifteen and had become a local preacher by eighteen, offered to go to America in response to Wesley's plea for preachers to travel there. The first chapter of American Methodism was about to be written.

It was a difficult time, since the War for American Independence was on the horizon. Most British preachers returned to England at the time of the Revolution, but Francis Asbury remained. He was the greatest of the circuit riders and became one of the best-known men across America. He has been called the "Prophet of the Long Road," a name that has sometimes been used to describe all circuit riders. His home was literally the open road and the saddle. The earliest Black evangelist in the colonies, Harry Hosier, whom Thomas Coke said was one of the best preachers in the world, was often a traveling companion of Asbury. As Asbury preached indoors, "Black Harry," as he was called, preached outside.

Eventually, an American Methodist church, independent from the Church of England, came into being. In 1784, Wesley, believing that as a presbyter of the Anglican Church he had a bishop's right to ordain, sent Thomas Coke as a superintendent of Methodists in America with instructions to consecrate Asbury to that same office. When Coke arrived in America, Asbury declined to accept the appointment as superintendent without an election by the preachers with whom he worked. This led to the famous Christmas Conference in Baltimore in 1784. It was at that conference that both Asbury and Coke were consecrated as general superintendents, a title that was later changed to bishop.

This same conference adopted a book of discipline, passed a resolution that prohibited Methodists from engaging in the slave trade, and established a college. A church was formally organized and named The Methodist Episcopal Church. The Articles of Religion and the Sunday Service, prepared by John Wesley for Methodists in America, were edited and adopted.

A Lasting Influence

John Wesley lived to be nearly eighty-eight years of age. Although he had married the widowed Mrs. Vazeille of London in 1751, his marriage proved to be an unhappy one. His preaching missions took him away from home over long periods of time. He traveled approximately five thousand miles a year for more than fifty years and preached more than forty thousand times. This "man of one book"[13] (the Bible), as Wesley called himself, was a prolific writer, translator, and editor. He published more than four hundred books and wrote numerous pamphlets and sermons. Many of his writings, including his *Journal*, have been preserved. Any money that came from his writings went to aid the work of the church. John Wesley died as he had lived most of his life, with the assurance that "the best of all is, God is with us." He is buried behind Wesley's Chapel on City Road in London, adjacent to the house where he spent his last years.

Of no less importance was the contribution of Charles Wesley to the Wesleyan movement. Charles composed thousands of hymns—hymns that set to music God's love and grace, hymns of assurance and praise. Among his lyrics are "Jesus, Lover of My Soul," "Love Divine, All Loves Excelling," "O For a Thousand Tongues to Sing," "Hark! the Herald Angels Sing," and "Christ the Lord Is Risen Today." His hymns have had a profound influence in helping to shape the faith of thousands of people. Sometimes his hymns held the early societies together when they had no preacher. Methodism became known as the singing church.

John and Charles Wesley always remained ministers in the Church of England. At the same time, they provided the impetus for the societies that eventually became The Methodist Church.

CHAPTER FOUR
OUR UNITED BRETHREN ROOTS

e now go to Germany to trace the ancestry of The United Brethren Church. About sixty miles north of Frankfurt is the town of Dillenburg, where Philip William Otterbein and his twin sister, Anna Margaret, who died in infancy, were born on June 3, 1726. Their father, John Daniel Otterbein, taught in the Latin School there. Two years later he resigned his teaching position to become the pastor of the Reformed churches in the neighboring communities of Frohnhausen and Wissenbach. The family moved to Frohnhausen, three miles north of Dillenburg.

In November of 1742, sorrow came to the Otterbein family. The father died at the age of forty-six. The mother, Wilhelmina Henrietta, with her six sons and one daughter, soon moved to Herborn, a few miles south, because she thought it would be less expensive to live there and would give the children an opportunity to attend the well-known German Reformed Herborn Academy, where their father had attended some years before. John Henry, the oldest son, was already a student there. Eventually, all six sons graduated from the Academy. As each son completed his training and began to earn a living, he helped his mother support the family.

Philip William Otterbein: Pastor and Missionary

Soon after his graduation from Herborn, Philip William was invited to teach at the Academy. The following year he was appointed pastor of the nearby village church at Ockersdorf that his brother John Henry had been serving. On June 13, 1749, he was ordained in the church at Dillenburg, where he had been baptized twenty-three years earlier.

In addition to teaching at the Academy, he was now preaching every Sunday and conducting weekly prayer meetings—something that was not common in those days. The fact that the prayer meetings were part of his responsibility indicates the strong pietistic emphasis placed on spirituality by the congregation, and in his own training, both at home and at the Academy.

But the young pastor had his problems. He attacked the formality of the church and stressed a high Christian moral conduct. Some in the congregation thought that he needed to curtail his zeal. He was too straightforward, too critical of their wrongdoing. Some of his parishioners went so far as to request the church authorities in Dillenburg and Herborn either to restrain him or to remove him. But the authorities refused to do either. When Philip William's mother heard of the opposition, she said, "Ah, William,…this place is too narrow for you." She was often heard to say, "My William will have to be a missionary; he is so frank, so open, so natural, so prophet-like."[1]

Little did Otterbein realize that within three years after he accepted his first pastoral appointment, he would be getting off a ship in New York harbor to begin a new ministry in Pennsylvania. It is estimated that at that time ninety thousand Germans were living in Pennsylvania, one-third of whom were related to The German Reformed Church. Many of them lived in communities without pastors or places of worship. For twenty years, appeals had come from America for more ministers.

The Reformed Church in Holland did much to support a Christian ministry among the Germans in Pennsylvania. They sent a pastor to America by the name of Michael Schlatter to supervise the work there. He returned to Holland after five years with an appeal for more missionaries and additional financial support. He was authorized to go into Germany to enlist six young men who were well educated and dedicated to missionary work. He went to the Herborn Academy and told his story to the faculty.

One of the six who responded was Philip William Otterbein, who was still a member of the faculty. Four others from Herborn signed up to go. The Academy recommended Otterbein as one who "always lived an honest, pious, and Christian life."[2] When the time came for him and his five companions to leave for Holland on their way to America, his widowed mother went to her room to cry and pray. When she came out, she pressed William's hand to her heart and said, "Go; the Lord bless thee and keep thee.... On earth I may not see thy face again—but go."[3]

The young men were examined at the Hague to determine their fitness for this kind of missionary undertaking. They set sail with Michael Schlatter in March and arrived in New York City on July 27, 1752. From there they went on to Philadelphia where congregations that knew of their coming issued calls to them. Otterbein accepted the call to go to Lancaster, Pennsylvania, a church that had been without a pastor for eighteen months. His assignment was for a five-year period.

A Spiritual Transformation

During Philip William Otterbein's ministry in Lancaster (perhaps his second year), he preached one Sunday on repentance and faith, one of his favorite themes. A man came up to him after the service and asked how he could experience God's grace in his own life. Otterbein paused for a moment, then replied, "My friend, advice is scarce with me today."[4] Then he walked away. His response burdened his heart. He prayed fervently, realizing that it was he who needed the grace he had preached about. He continued to pray until he came to an inner assurance of God's grace within his own life.

It was a turning point in his ministry that he always regarded as singularly important. From then on, he preached about the need to experience God's forgiveness. His preaching became more confident and convincing. He no longer read his sermons; he turned away from traditional formalities; and he put aside the silk robe he wore in the pulpit.

Otterbein served the Lancaster church six years; then he moved on to Tulpehocken. In addition to preaching on Sunday, he continued the practice he had followed in Germany of holding midweek prayer services. They were among the first ever held in America. Every week he went from house to house, reading the Bible, singing hymns, and praying with families. His ministry was beginning to extend to other communities without pastoral leadership. He even went as far as Frederick, Maryland, more than one hundred miles away, to preach in the church there that was without a pastor.

Facing Opposition

In 1760, Otterbein accepted a call to go to the Reformed Church in Frederick. During his second year there, he married Susan LeRoy from his former parish in Lancaster.

His preaching continued to be forthright. Some gladly heard his message of living a pure and godly life, but others opposed him. Dissatisfaction continued to mount until a majority of the members decided to have him dismissed. On one occasion, they locked the church door against him. When the congregation gathered the following Sunday, some of his supporters were ready to force the door open. But Otterbein would not permit a forced entry. He said, "If I am not permitted to enter the church peaceably, I can and will preach here in the graveyard."[5] He stood on one of the tombstones and delivered his sermon, much like John Wesley had done in Epworth about twenty years earlier. He announced that services would be held from the same place the following Sunday. By that time the opposition had backed down and opened up the church. In spite of this episode, a fine stone church and parsonage were built in Frederick while he was a pastor there.

After being in Frederick five years, Philip and Susan moved back to Pennsylvania, to York where the congregation had been without a regular pastor for two years.

Otterbein's interest in reaching people beyond his own congregation continued. His travels brought him in contact with other pastors who shared his concern for preaching a message of personal salvation. Meetings beyond the local church were sometimes held in groves, or wherever large numbers of people could assemble. People from miles around came, bringing provisions to last several days. They spent the nights in nearby homes, in barns, or in makeshift shelters. Sometimes preachers from different denominations preached at the same time in different locations—wherever a crowd gathered.

Martin Boehm, a Mennonite, was one such preacher. When chosen by lot to be a pastor—typical of Mennonite practice—he felt distressed because he thought he would not be good at preaching. But believing the lot represented a divine selection, he accepted the appointment. While preaching grace and the way of salvation to others, he realized his own spiritual poverty. One day while plowing, he knelt down in the middle of the field and cried out, "Lord, save [me]. I am lost!" His heart was touched by the words of Jesus, "I am come to seek and to save that which is lost."[6] He sprang to his feet, filled with an inner joy, and went to tell his wife.

"We Are Brethren!"

Once, Otterbein came from York to attend a service held in a barn on the farm of Isaac Long, six miles northeast of Lancaster. Martin Boehm, whom Otterbein had never met, was preaching. Otterbein was greatly moved by Boehm's witness to the gospel. Boehm spoke of a spiritual struggle and of an experience of Christian assurance similar to his own. At the end of the sermon, Otterbein went up to Boehm, threw his arms around him, and exclaimed in German, "Wir sind Brüder!" ("We are brethren!").

What a contrast of personalities: Otterbein was six feet tall; Boehm was short with a white beard. Otterbein was highly educated; Boehm had little formal education. Otterbein represented an established Old World church; Boehm represented a persecuted sect. But they were of one heart and brothers in Christ. That meeting in the barn on a Whitsunday was a significant moment in the history of the Church of the United Brethren in Christ. From that time on, Otterbein and Boehm became close friends and coworkers in the revitalization of their respective churches. Boehm was eventually excommunicated from his Mennonite Church because it was feared that his enthusiasm and association with people of other religious persuasions could cause a division within its ranks.

Otterbein's life was soon touched with sorrow. Susan died in 1768 after a lingering illness. They had been married only six years, and there is no record of children having been born to them. Philip William remained single the rest of his life.

Two years after Susan's death, Otterbein returned to Germany to see his mother and five brothers. Four of his brothers were serving churches, and his next oldest brother, John Charles, was teaching at the Herborn Academy. Otterbein returned to York after a nine- to ten-month visit. It was his first and last trip to his homeland.

Otterbein's Last Church

In 1773, Otterbein received a call from a German Reformed Church in Baltimore that had split off from the original congregation over divided loyalties centering around a former pastor. The group that had pulled away wanted Otterbein as their pastor. Those who had oversight of the Reformed churches counseled him against accepting the call, so at first he declined the church's invitation. The pastor who had served the congregation following the split was acquainted with Francis Asbury, the Methodist evangelist of Baltimore. He suggested to Asbury that he write to Otterbein to urge him to reconsider. Asbury's letter prompted Otterbein to rethink his decision. After much prayerful thought, he decided to accept the call in spite of the disapproval of his denominational leaders.

Otterbein began his pastorate in Baltimore on May 4, 1774, shortly before the American Revolution. His concern for a revival of faith within The German Reformed Church was shared by other Reformed pastors who called themselves the United Ministers. In 1784, ten years after he went to Baltimore, he was invited to the Christmas Conference called by the Methodists to participate in the consecration of Francis Asbury as bishop.

The lay preachers who looked to Otterbein and Boehm for guidance met at the farm of Frederick Kemp and his son Peter near Frederick, Maryland, on September 25, 1800, and adopted the name United Brethren in Christ. At that conference, both Otterbein and Boehm were elected superintendents, or bishops. It marked the origin of the first denomination to be born on American soil.

Although loosely organized, the "Otterbein People," as they were called, expanded their work into German settlements through Appalachia, into Pennsylvania, Ohio, Maryland, Virginia, and Kentucky. Following the death of Martin Boehm on March 23, 1812, Otterbein, who was almost eighty-six years of age, thought that the time had come to ordain others. He ordained three men to the ministry, one of whom was Christian Newcomer.

When Otterbein died on November 17, 1813, he was still a pastor of the Reformed Church; yet, he was setting into motion, along with Martin Boehm and other coworkers, a new denomination. On hearing of Otterbein's death, Asbury said, "Is Father Otterbein dead? Great and good man of God! An honor to his church and country. One of the greatest scholars and divines that ever came to America, or born in it."[7] Otterbein is buried just outside the Baltimore church where he preached for more than thirty-nine years. He left almost no written records. It is said that because of his modesty, he destroyed most of his papers during the last year of his life.

Association With the Methodists

The similarities between the Otterbein and Wesley families are striking. Both were large families: Seven out of ten Otterbein children and ten out of nineteen Wesley children grew to maturity. Both fathers were pastors. Both mothers had a profound influence on the spiritual and educational development of their children. All the sons of both families became pastors. Herborn Academy was to the Otterbeins what Oxford University was to the Wesleys. Philip William Otterbein and John and Charles Wesley all maintained their clerical relationships with the churches in which they had been ordained. None of them set out to begin a new denomination, but the groups that emerged as a result of their ministry became distinct churches: the Church of the United Brethren in Christ and The Methodist Church.

The United Brethren and Methodist associations were numerous. Francis Asbury was instrumental in Otterbein's going to Baltimore. Otterbein participated in the consecration of Asbury. Martin Boehm joined a Methodist society after leaving the Mennonite Church and offered his home as a preaching place. Asbury preached the funeral of Boehm and spoke words of praise for Otterbein after Otterbein's death. Martin Boehm's son Henry was a traveling preaching companion to Asbury.

The Methodists and the "Otterbein People" held to a similar doctrine and church organization. Their preachers often joined forces in their evangelistic work, one group preaching in German and the other in English. The Wesley-Asbury groups were often called "English Methodists," while the Otterbein-Boehm and Albright groups were called "German (or Dutch) Methodists." They proclaimed a common message: new life in Christ. It is the good news, a priceless heritage, that we still claim today as United Methodists.

CHAPTER FIVE

OUR EVANGELICAL ROOTS

e now turn to our Evangelical origins. Drummer boy turned preacher and founder of The Evangelical Church— so was Jacob Albright. He was born of parents with a German ancestry near Pottstown, Pennsylvania, in 1759. He was baptized, took catechism instruction, and became a member of The Lutheran Church.

Jacob was seventeen when the Declaration of Independence was signed in 1776. He signed up to serve in the Revolution as a drummer in the Pennsylvania militia.

When Jacob was twenty-six, with the war behind him, he married Catherine Cope. They purchased a farm in eastern Lancaster County that had a rich deposit of limestone and clay. In addition to farming the land, Jacob set up a kiln and used the clay to make roof tile and bricks. He was a conscientious worker and a good businessman. Known as "the Honest Tilemaker," Jacob prospered. Everything seemed to go well with him, at least outwardly; yet, he confessed, "[I] lived as though the little span of duration would last eternally.... I was not really happy."[1]

Soon, a great tragedy came to Jacob and Catherine. Several of their children died in an epidemic of dysentery in 1790. Jacob's spiritual unrest and the death of his children seemed to conspire against him. The indifference he had felt toward religion and the church only added to his burden. He turned for counsel to Anthony Houtz, the German Reformed pastor who had conducted the children's funerals. He also turned to his neighbor Isaac Davies, who was a Methodist lay preacher, and to Adam Riegel, a lay preacher of The United Brethren Church.

A Spiritual Awakening

The following year, Jacob's life bordered on despair. He said, "How deeply I regretted my past life, and how widely different I would have lived could I have lived it over again!"[2] During the summer, he attended a prayer meeting in the home of his neighbor Adam Riegel. It was there that he poured out his heart to God, confessed his unworthiness, and experienced a spiritual rebirth: "All fear and anxiety of heart disappeared. Joy and blessed peace inbreathed my breast. God gave witness to my spirit that I had become a child of God."[3] It was a turning point in Albright's life. The experience not only spoke to his own needs but prompted a concern for the spiritual welfare of his friends and neighbors.

Soon, he felt the need to be nurtured in his newfound faith. He turned to the Methodists who met in the home of his neighbor Isaac Davies. Albright wrote:

> At this time I knew of no association of Christians who seemed to be more zealous and active, and whose *Discipline* and regulations suited me better, than the Methodists. For this reason I united with them and found among them opportunity to receive great blessings and benefit for my soul. As many things in their mode of worship were not yet clear to me, since it was conducted in the English language, with which I was not sufficiently familiar at this time, I earnestly endeavored to become acquainted with their doctrine and *Discipline,* with which I was much pleased. I conformed to its regulations in my conduct and devotions.[4]

Before long the Methodists granted Albright an exhorter's license. His Methodist friends encouraged him to go out as an itinerant preacher, but he felt unqualified to do that at this stage in his Christian experience. Furthermore, the Methodists worked among English-speaking people, and he was aware of his limitations with the language. Soon, his reluctance to preach was broken by the assurance that God's grace was sufficient to sustain him in spite of all his limitations.

Jacob began preaching in the fall of 1796. Because he was gone from home and from the Methodist class meetings for long periods of time, his affiliations with the Methodists began to lapse. He let his Methodist exhorter's license expire, as he was turning more and more to the German-speaking communities.

The Problems of a Traveling Preacher

Before long, Jacob was preaching in all the surrounding counties of Pennsylvania. He also went into Maryland and Virginia. He preached in churches, homes, barns, and schoolhouses; in the woods and open fields; along the street—wherever people assembled. His preaching engendered enthusiastic support as well as angry opposition. He was often blunt and somewhat argumentative. He especially antagonized the people who belonged to the established churches. He emphasized a life-changing Christian experience rather than formal adherence to a creed, or simply receiving the sacraments.

Jacob's travels continued to take him away from Catherine and his family. He would mold the tile and bricks and leave them to be fired and sold by Catherine and the children. Rumors began to circulate that this "fanatic" was not taking proper care of his family and shouldering his share of responsibility. Catherine did not appreciate his long absences, and Jacob thought he did not have the full support of his family. Two of the highest claims in Jacob's life, the call of God to go out to preach and his responsibility to his family, were warring against each other.

More and more people responded to Albright's preaching. His followers were often ridiculed as "knee-sliders," "head-hangers," "groaners," "fanatics," and even "hypocrites." Their designation as "German Methodists" was mild compared with other epithets. Yet, all of this did not stop Jacob. He brought together a number of converts who were living in three different communities in 1800 and formed three classes. The groups were organized after the pattern of the Methodist class meeting to which he had belonged. A class leader was appointed for each group.

At the conference held in November 1803, the classes declared themselves a church organization. It was at their first annual conference in 1807 that the title of bishop was bestowed on Jacob Albright. The conference asked him to prepare a statement of discipline patterned after the Methodist *Discipline*. That task, however, had to be completed by his friend George Miller because of Jacob's failing health. The conference assumed the name Newly-Formed Methodist Conference, although it had no formal ties with The Methodist Church. The name did reveal, however, the influence the Methodist class meetings had on Albright and his appreciation for Methodist doctrine and discipline.

Albright's Last Days

Jacob continued to preach and to supervise the classes, which by this time had taken on the character of a church. But his health continued to decline. Accompanied by two friends from a preaching mission east of Harrisburg, he arrived at Kleinfeltersville, fifteen miles from his home, when he could go no farther. They stopped at the home of George Becker where a room was kept for traveling preachers. Jacob said, "Have you my bed ready? I have come to die."[5] During the few weeks that he lingered, he gave encouragement to the friends about him and thanked God for the grace that had sustained him on his Christian pilgrimage. Jacob's wife was notified, but she and his daughter did not arrive until after he had died.

Jacob Albright died on May 18, 1808, at only forty-nine years of age. The tuberculosis he had contracted years earlier had been aggravated by his exposure to all kinds of weather. He was buried in the Becker family cemetery on their farm. In 1850, The Evangelical Church built a memorial chapel near his grave. Ten years later, a more permanent church was erected. It still stands today.

In 1816, eight years after Albright's death, the "Albright People" or "The So-Called Albrights" took the name of The Evangelical Association. It was The Evangelical Church that came together with The United Brethren Church in 1946 to form The Evangelical United Brethren Church. That denomination merged with The Methodist Church to form The United Methodist Church in 1968.

Association With the Methodists and United Brethren

The Evangelical Church had a close relationship to The Methodist Church from the very beginning. Albright joined a Methodist class and was granted a preacher's license. The early Evangelical conference was called The Newly-Formed Methodist Conference. Their first *Discipline* borrowed heavily from the Methodist *Discipline* and Articles of Faith.

Two years after Albright's death, John Dreisbach, a young man twenty-one years of age and a close friend of Albright, was encouraged by Francis Asbury to join the ranks of the Methodists. At that time Asbury thought the German language would soon become extinct in America. He believed that the cause of the Evangelicals could best be served if they would not confine their work to the German-speaking people. Dreisbach made a counterproposal that Asbury create German circuits and conferences, thereby making it possible to be "one people." But Bishop Asbury thought that would not be expedient. This early overture toward union would be repeated on later occasions.

The Evangelical Church also had a close relationship with The United Brethren Church. Both groups worked among the German-speaking people. Albright's spiritual rebirth occurred in a prayer meeting among the United Brethren in the home of Adam Riegel. Five years after Albright's death, both groups sent representatives to the home of John Walter to discuss the possibility of union. And at their General Conference in 1816, The Evangelical Association considered a proposal to unite with The United Brethren Church.

Jacob Albright preached only twelve years. More than three hundred converts began their journey of faith under his preaching. His contribution is best summarized in his last admonition to those who worked with him:

> In all you do or intend to do, let it be your aim to promote the honor and glory of God, and to promulgate and exalt the operations of his grace…and be faithful coworkers with them in the path which the Lord has shown unto you, and he will grant you his blessing.[6]

CHAPTER SIX

TWO CENTURIES OF MINISTRY

I t has been said that when John Wesley died he left behind one silver spoon, a worn-out clergyman's coat, a much-abused reputation, and The Methodist Church.

Not unlike Wesley, Otterbein, Boehm, and Albright left behind them a movement that would eventually become The Evangelical United Brethren Church. Those who knew Jacob Albright said that his death "had the tendency to induce preachers and people to consecrate themselves more fully to God's work."[1] And it was said of Asbury and Otterbein that they stood for what they called "sensible religion.... They contended that religion was...a personal, conscious, experienced relationship with the living God."[2]

From each of these pioneers, claimed by God, we have received a rich heritage, a heritage that has touched almost every aspect of our lives. Since the beginning days of the Oxford "Methodists," the "Otterbein People," and the "Albright People," the church that came into being through their influence has served a multitude of people all over the world and has grown to millions of members today. What are some of the areas of ministry during these past two centuries that have influenced the lives of so many of us today?

The United Methodist Church today represents most ethnic backgrounds, including those who speak most of the world's languages. Black Americans, for instance, have always played a significant role in the drama of Methodism. They were present at the Christmas Conference in 1784. Such early Black evangelists as Harry Hosier, Henry

Evans, Peter Williams, and John Stewart (a missionary to the Wyandot Indians) will always occupy important places in the annals of our history.

Education and Publishing

From the time Wesley founded Kingswood School near Bristol, England, to the present, education has been a major concern of the people called Methodists. Even prior to Wesley's death, Methodist colleges were being founded in the colonies. By the time of the Civil War, Methodism had established thirty-four colleges that have continued into our own era. Today, 123 colleges, universities, seminaries, professional and secondary schools maintain ties with The United Methodist Church. Among these, including schools that were formerly Evangelical United Brethren institutions, are thirteen seminaries and eleven Black colleges. Meharry Medical College in Nashville, Tennessee, has graduated fifteen percent of all Black physicians and dentists in this country. Wesleyan College in Macon, Georgia, founded in 1836, was the first women's college in America.

The Sunday school has long been an integral part of our church. Hannah Ball, a Methodist preacher, had a Sunday school for children as early as 1770. The Methodist Sunday School Union was established in 1827. Today, more than half a million teachers, leaders, and administrators are engaged in the educational ministries of our churches. Each year approximately four hundred curriculum resources are published.

The Methodist Book Concern was founded in 1789 in Philadelphia. The circuit riders carried the books and tracts published by the Book Concern in their saddlebags to spread among the people along their circuits.

Not unlike the early Methodists, the Evangelical United Brethren were keenly aware of the crucial role of Christian education and the religious press. Bishop Seybert loaded his carriage with books and study materials and distributed them among the preachers and the church members wherever he traveled. Otterbein knew that Bible study and catechetical training were indispensable for Christian nurture. Sunday schools were in existence in both denominations as early as 1832.

The Evangelical and the United Brethren churches entered the publishing enterprise shortly after they were formally organized. The Evangelicals named a book agent as early as 1816. The Evangelical Press in Harrisburg, Pennsylvania, and the Otterbein Press in Dayton,

Ohio, served the churches. In addition to these publishing firms, there were publishing houses in Stuttgart, Germany, and Berne, Switzerland, and a number of bookstores.

From these humble beginnings, the publishing enterprise has grown into The United Methodist Publishing House, located in Nashville, Tennessee. In addition to the curriculum resources produced, approximately 175 books are published each year.

Missionary Outreach and Social Concerns

Methodism caught early the vision of Christ's command to "go therefore and make disciples of all nations" (Matthew 28:19). Lay preachers and their families, influenced by the Wesleyan Revival in England, came to America; Thomas Coke was en route to a mission field when he died at sea; the circuit riders were our missionaries on horseback to the frontier settlers. In the tradition of Bishop Asbury, Bishop William McKendree traveled tirelessly in establishing The Methodist Church. Frontier preachers, such as Peter Cartwright, won countless numbers of converts.

Frontier evangelistic work was also carried out by the Evangelicals and the United Brethren. Revivals and camp meetings were very much a part of their Christian witness. Christian Newcomer, an early United Brethren bishop, crossed the Allegheny Mountains on horseback forty-eight times, making his last trip in 1829 when he was eighty years old. Bishop John Seybert of The Evangelical Church made numerous trips on horseback and in his wagon from Pennsylvania to Ohio, Iowa, Illinois, Michigan, Wisconsin, Missouri, New York, New Jersey, and up into Canada.

Early in the nineteenth century our Methodist, Evangelical, and United Brethren forebears caught the vision of a worldwide mission of evangelism, education, and service. The Evangelical and United Brethren branches were both mission-minded from the beginning and pushed out beyond the borders of the United States. By 1841, both The United Brethren Church and The Evangelical Association had organized mission societies. Women's societies were organized to support the work of the mission. The first missionary venture outside the country was across the border to the north into Canada. John Dreisbach, an Evangelical preacher, crossed the Niagara River in 1816 and preached in the German settlements just north of it. By the mid-1840's both of these German-speaking denominations were sending missionaries to Germany, an endeavor in which the Methodists also joined. In 1968, at the time of union, The Evangelical United Brethren Church had 145 missionaries under appointment in world missions. Their Women's Society for World Service was a strong force.

In 1740, George Whitefield was instrumental in bringing into being the Bethesda Orphanage in Savannah, Georgia. It represents Methodism's early engagement in ministering to the sick, the aged, the homeless children, and other needy people. The Evangelical United Brethren Church supported eleven orphanages for children and youth, homes for the elderly, and other institutions to meet human need at the time they united with The Methodist Church in 1968. Today, there are many hospitals and homes throughout the country that are owned and operated by The United Methodist Church.

The women of the church have long been one of the strongest support groups for mission work, both at home and abroad. They have given financial support and conducted study programs related to national and world missions. Today, the United Methodist Women have a special concern for the spiritual development and empowerment of women. Our United Methodist Men affirm the centrality of Christ in the lives of men and in all their relationships as their primary purpose.

By 1889, the General Conference of The United Brethren Church made it possible for women to be ordained, even though several women who had felt called to the ministry had sought pastoral recognition as far back as 1841.

The Methodist Church has long been a champion of human dignity and social justice. John Wesley himself opposed slavery, child labor, and the liquor traffic. He was interested in prison reform. Our church today continually seeks ways to help make our society more loving and just. The General Conference of 1908 adopted our influential Social Creed. Such global issues as peace and justice, human rights, hunger, and poverty challenge us to prayer and study, advocacy and action in the spirit of Christ. We are concerned not only with world problems but also with the needs of people in our own communities. How can we individually, and as a congregation, help alleviate suffering and hardship, discrimination and injustice?

Over the years we have been challenged to be in mission. We have been called to bear witness to the gospel of Jesus Christ by word and deed through evangelism, teaching, healing, and a wide variety of helping ministries. Today, our United Methodist Church is reaching out to people everywhere. The mission of each congregation has been enlarged by our global connections, which include an active partnership with our United Methodist central conferences overseas and the autonomous Methodist churches in other countries.

Ecumenical Outreach

It was said of John Wesley that he was "the most ecumenically minded of all the great reformers."[3] In his sermon on the "Catholic Spirit," he quoted 2 Kings 10:15: "Is thine heart right, as my heart is with thy heart?... If it be, give me thine hand."[4] That catholic spirit has been expressed in the lives of many Methodist leaders. Notable among them was the late John R. Mott, a layman who believed that Christians belong together and that we must affirm that we are followers of one Christ.

Likewise, Otterbein's Reformed Church was rooted in a tradition that emphasized the unity of the church. The Evangelical United Brethren Church, as well as the Methodist, has assumed a prominent role in ecumenical affairs. Our United Methodist Constitution states:

> As part of the church universal, The United Methodist Church believes that the Lord of the church is calling Christians everywhere to strive toward unity; and therefore it will seek, and work for, unity at all levels of church life: through world relationships with other Methodist churches and united churches related to The Methodist Church or The Evangelical United Brethren Church, through councils of churches, and through plans of union and covenantal relationships with churches of Methodist or other denominational traditions.[5]

Division, Unity, and Challenge

Not long after the deaths of Charles and John Wesley, the newly formed Methodist Episcopal Church in America faced division within. One group pulled away over the authority of bishops. The slave issue prompted the formation of the African Methodist Episcopal Church in 1816 under the leadership of Richard Allen and The African Methodist

Episcopal Church Zion in 1821. The Methodist Protestant Church was formed in 1830 by those who wanted more lay leadership. The slave issue was also instrumental in the formation of The Wesleyan Methodist Connection in 1843, and The Methodist Episcopal Church, South, in 1845. The Free Methodist Church was organized in 1860 and The Colored Methodist Episcopal Church in 1870 by groups of Black Methodists.

A uniting conference held in 1939, in Kansas City, Missouri, marked the formation of The Methodist Church through the union of The Methodist Protestant Church, The Methodist Episcopal Church, and The Methodist Episcopal Church, South. The other churches that had grown out of The Methodist Episcopal Church continued as separate groups; yet, all claim a Wesleyan heritage. Today, the World Methodist Council links 74 member denominations that claim a Wesleyan heritage. With some 36 million members, these Wesleyan churches are found in 130 countries.

By 1889, The United Brethren Church found itself in the midst of a schism. The majority of the members favored the development of a new constitution and a modification of their Confession of Faith. They also wanted lay representation at their General Conference. And, they would permit membership in secret societies so long as it did not infringe on the rights of those outside the organization, become injurious to the character of its members, and was not contrary to the Word of God. But a minority disagreed. Led by Bishop Milton Wright, the father of Orville and Wilbur Wright, the opposition formed a new church known as The United Brethren Church (Old Constitution). They have continued as a separate denomination.

The Evangelical Church also experienced division. The church divided in 1891 into The Evangelical Association and The United Evangelical Church, but they reunited in 1922 to form The Evangelical Church.

For more than a century, the United Brethren and the Evangelical churches explored the possibility of becoming a single denomination. But it was not until 1946 in Johnstown, Pennsylvania, that The Evangelical United Brethren Church came into being.

When The Evangelical United Brethren Church united with The Methodist Church in 1968 at Dallas, Texas, to form The United Methodist Church, the Evangelical United Brethren congregations in North America had a membership of about 750,000. That compared

Roots of The United Methodist Church in America

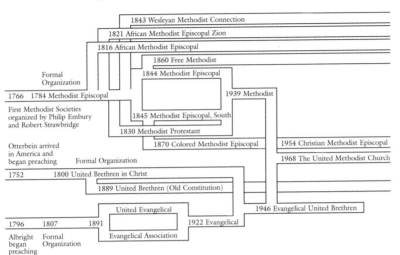

with a Methodist membership of more than ten million. It represented a ratio of almost fourteen to one. Notwithstanding the potential problems and fears of such an imbalance, the intervening years have given us cause to thank God that we are united in Christ. Concluding the uniting service in the Dallas Municipal Auditorium, April 23, 1968, the congregation joined in a prayer that unites us today:

> We are no longer our own, but Thine. Put us to what Thou wilt, rank us with whom Thou wilt, put us to doing, put us to suffering: let us be employed for Thee or laid aside by Thee, exalted for Thee or brought low for Thee: let us be full, let us be empty: let us have all things, let us have nothing. We freely and heartily yield all things to Thy pleasure and disposal.
>
> And now, 0 gracious and blessed God, Father, Son and Holy Spirit, Thou art ours and we are Thine. So be it. And the covenant which we have made on earth, let it be ratified in heaven. Amen.[6]

John Wesley's words toward the close of his life continue to speak to all who claim to be his spiritual descendants:

I am not afraid that the people called Methodists should ever cease to exist either in Europe or America. But I am afraid, lest they should only exist as a dead sect, having the form of religion without the power. And this undoubtedly will be the case, unless they hold fast both the doctrine, spirit, and discipline with which they first set out.[7]

CHAPTER SEVEN

WHAT WE BELIEVE

ords, however carefully chosen, never seem to express adequately all that I believe. Somehow the mind does not speak the language of the heart. New understandings constantly reveal to me a dimension of my faith I had not given serious thought to before. Many aspects of the Christian faith are still a mystery to me. I "see in a mirror, dimly." I am awaiting further light. I trust, realizing there is truth embodied in what I do not fully understand. But I rejoice in the fact that I can still grow in my understanding of the faith. I invite you to think seriously about what it is you believe and to discuss your beliefs with others. I invite you to join me in exploring the major beliefs of The United Methodist Church.

Our *Discipline* says: "The pioneers in the traditions that flowed together into The United Methodist Church understood themselves as standing in the central stream of Christian spirituality and doctrine, loyal heirs of the authentic Christian tradition."[1] But they also believed that no single doctrine could ever completely express God's eternal Word. They affirmed the ancient creeds and confessions as "valid summaries of Christian truth."[2] Yet, they did not regard them as the final authority or as ultimate standards for testing the truth or error of Christian doctrine. They insisted, however, that there are fundamental truths at the heart of the gospel that can be identified and must be preserved. How do we, as United Methodists, go about discovering these truths? Where do we turn to claim "a faith that will not shrink, though pressed by every foe"?[3]

Four Guidelines

Our United Methodist *Discipline* states:

> As United Methodists, we have an obligation to bear a faithful
> Christian witness to Jesus Christ, the living reality at the center of
> the Church's life and witness. To fulfill this obligation, we reflect
> critically on our biblical and theological inheritance, striving to
> express faithfully the witness we make in our own time.
>
> Two considerations are central to this endeavor: the sources
> from which we derive our theological affirmations and the cri-
> teria by which we assess the adequacy of our understanding
> and witness.
>
> Wesley believed that the living core of the Christian faith was
> revealed in Scripture, illumined by tradition, vivified in personal
> experience, and confirmed by reason.[4]

1. *Scripture.* The Bible is the primary source for what we believe. Our
   doctrines are grounded in the biblical story of God's self-disclosure
   in creation; in the life, death, and resurrection of Jesus Christ; in the
   activity of the Holy Spirit; and in the coming of God's promised
   kingdom. We believe that God's Word and will are revealed to us
   when Scripture is interpreted in light of its original message, as well
   as in terms of its meaning for us today. "As we open our minds and
   hearts to the Word of God through the words of human beings
   inspired by the Holy Spirit, faith is born and nourished, our understanding is deepened, and the possibilities for transforming the
   world become apparent to us."[5]

2. *Tradition.* Our Christian tradition is rooted in the lives and within
   the works and testimony of those who have gone before us. Church
   ritual, creeds, and hymns are all part of our heritage. The devotional
   classics and theological writings of Christian men and women over
   the centuries form an important part of our tradition. Christian art
   also illumines the sacred story. The lives of the saints, people we read
   about in books as well as those we have known personally, bear testimony to the faith. Our tradition gives us an insight into how earlier
   Christians and communities of faith understood God's will, how
   they interpreted the gospel, and how they applied the Scripture to
   their own life situations.

3. *Christian experience.* Our personal experience of God's pardoning and healing love is radically different from intellectual assent to the message of the Bible or to doctrines set forth in our creeds.

Christian experience [new life in Christ] gives us new eyes to see the living truth in Scripture. It confirms the biblical message for our present. It illumines our understanding of God and creation and motivates us to make sensitive moral judgments. Although profoundly personal, Christian experience is also corporate; our theological task is informed by the experience of the church and by the common experiences of all humanity. In our attempts to understand the biblical message, we recognize that God's gift of liberating love embraces the whole of creation.[6]

4. *Reason.* We believe that all truth comes from God. Doctrines that are developed by the study of Scripture, in light of tradition and Christian experience, commend themselves to thoughtful people and are submitted to critical analysis. Our beliefs must take into account scientific knowledge and practical experience and avoid self-contradiction. We should try to discover the relationship of revelation to reason, faith to science, and grace to nature as we endeavor to develop doctrines that are credible and clear.

We believe these four guidelines are to be brought to bear on all doctrinal considerations. They should interact and be used in combination with one another, always remembering the primacy of Scripture. Each of the four guidelines enriches the others. Each brings its unique perspective. Taken together, these four guidelines help us clarify what we believe.

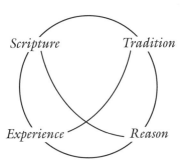

Scripture   *Tradition*

Experience   *Reason*

United Methodists accept the historic creeds and confessions as cherished testimonies of our Christian past. But we also encourage new statements of old truths. Many of the truths we affirm as United Methodists are shared by other Christians.

Our Essential Beliefs

You will want to think through these essential beliefs for yourself and will have your own statements of faith to make. What do you believe about God, for instance, that you would tell a friend? What questions remain unanswered? Are there certain understandings of God that cause you problems? I invite you to respond to each of the beliefs that follow.

1. *God.* We believe in one God, who is infinite in wisdom, power, and love. We affirm our trust in God as the Creator, Sustainer, and Ruler of all things, the One who comes to us as the Holy Spirit. We believe that the life, death, and resurrection of Jesus Christ give us a clear, full, and true revelation of God. We believe that "God is spirit" (John 4:24). No one has ever seen God. God is love. "If we love one another, God lives in us" (1 John 4:12). We believe that God is all-merciful, righteous, and just. Through prayer, and in fellowship with God, we grow in our understanding of the divine purpose and will for our lives.

2. *Jesus Christ.* We believe in Jesus, the Christ—the promised Messiah and Deliverer, our Savior, and the Savior of the world. We believe that Jesus lived a life that was truly human and truly divine. He was tempted in every respect as we are, yet without sinning (Hebrews 4:15-16). He lived in perfect obedience to God. The unmatched depth of God's love is revealed within the life and ministry of Jesus' preaching, teaching, and healing, and in his suffering, death, and res- urrection. We affirm the faith of the early Christians that Jesus Christ is the Lord. We believe that the living Christ is present with us and that through faith in Christ we experience the joy of salvation.

3. *Holy Spirit.* We believe in the Holy Spirit as God present with us for guidance, comfort, and strength. We affirm the Holy Spirit's presence in our lives, inspiring those qualities known in the New Testament as "the fruit of the Spirit...love, joy, peace, patience, kindness, generosity, faithfulness, gentleness, and self-control" (Galatians 5:22-23). Likewise, the Holy Spirit inspires gifts that are

to be used for our mutual upbuilding: "To each is given the manifestation of the Spirit for the common good" (1 Corinthians 12:7). "The Spirit helps us in our weakness" (Romans 8:26) and keeps us in perpetual remembrance of the truth of Christ.

4. *Forgiveness.* We believe in the reality of sin and in the forgiveness of sin: "If we say that we have no sin, we deceive ourselves, and the truth is not in us. If we confess our sins, [God] who is faithful and just will forgive us our sins and cleanse us from all unrighteousness" (1 John 1:8-9). We confess that we have alienated ourselves from God by our self-centeredness and disobedience. Our estrangement thwarts our hopes of achieving what is good. We believe that the Holy Spirit quickens our conscience, convicts us of sin, and prompts us toward righteousness. Our repentance is matched by God's gracious love and acceptance. Forgiveness re-establishes a broken relationship and enables us to begin again. Just as God forgives us, we are expected to forgive others.

5. *Scripture.* We believe that the Word of God contained in the Old and New Testaments is "the sufficient rule, both of our faith and practice."[7] Although God is revealed in many ways, we believe that the testimony of the Bible is crucial in helping us live in terms of God's will. We believe that the Bible was written by people who were inspired and challenged by the Spirit of God. The Bible is a record of the many experiences men and women had on their journey of faith: faithfulness and disobedience, high commitments and broken promises, affirmation and doubt. We believe that God speaks to us through the Scripture when we interpret the ancient witness in light of both its original meaning and its message for us today.

6. *Church.* We believe in the church as a community of faith and love and as a fellowship for worship, study, and service of all who are united to the living Lord. The church is more than a place, a building, and an institution. The church is present when we come together as a gathered community, as well as when we express our faith in witness and service in the world about us. We confess that "the church's one foundation is Jesus Christ her Lord."[8] We affirm our belief in the church universal: the fellowship of Christians around the world. This is what The Apostles' Creed means when it refers to "the holy catholic church." We recognize that within the fellowship of the

church are those who have lived and died before us, who have finished their course in faith and who now rest from their labors.

7. *Kingdom of God.* We believe in the kingdom of God as the divine rule in human society. One of Jesus' favorite themes was the kingdom of God. It represented for him God's reign, the manifestation of God's purpose and will. Many of his parables about the Kingdom depict God as One who searches for us. Jesus spoke of the Kingdom in various ways: within us, around us, among us, beyond us. The Kingdom is already here; it is yet to come. It is a present reality; it is a future hope. We are called into fellowship with God and with one another to the end that the divine will can be expressed in and through us. We pray, "Thy kingdom come, thy will be done on earth as it is in heaven."[9]

8. *Eternal life.* We believe in the final triumph of righteousness and in the life everlasting. We have here, through faith in Christ, a glimpse of that which shall be revealed. We believe that eternal life is not simply an extension of life beyond death, but it is also a quality of life in Christ lived here and now. To live in Christ is to know eternal life. Even though we "walk through the darkest valley," we fear no evil. Although we may have questions about what life after death may be like, we are confident that the promise of Christ is trustworthy and that God will be with us and sustain us.

Emphases of Special Importance for United Methodists

In addition to the foregoing statements of faith, there are other emphases that have a special significance for United Methodists.

9. *Human dignity.* We believe that God endows each person with dignity and moral responsibility. The alienation and discrimination many individuals feel is painful to them and to us. We seek to be sensitive to each person's longing for self-respect and the desire of all people to share in a good life. Our clearest insight into what human dignity means is found in Jesus Christ, who brings together into one life the truly human and the truly divine. We recognize our responsibility to God and to one another.

10. *Grace.* We believe in the primacy of grace. Grace is God's self-giving love bestowed on us quite apart from our having deserved it. God's love is freely given to us, not because we have earned it, but because we need it. "We acknowledge God's prevenient grace, the divine love that surrounds all humanity and precedes any and all of our conscious impulses. This grace prompts our first wish to please God, our first glimmer of understanding concerning God's will, and our 'first slight transient conviction' of having sinned against God."[10]

11. *Conversion.* We believe that a decisive change in our lives can and does occur, prompted by grace and by the guidance of the Holy Spirit. This new birth, or conversion, "may be sudden and dramatic, or gradual and cumulative. It marks a new beginning, yet it is part of an ongoing process. Christian experience as personal transformation always expresses itself as faith working by love."[11]

We may look back on our lives and identify a time, place, or series of experiences that we recognize as a turning point or as transforming moments in our conversion. There is also a sense in which we need to be daily transformed and renewed by the Spirit of Christ. Our salvation is not static. It is not simply an experience of the past. When conversion is viewed as a dynamic encounter with the living God, we can say, "I was saved, I am being saved, I shall always need to be saved." We must always be receptive to the leading of the Holy Spirit.

12. *Faith and works.* We believe that faith and good works belong together. What we believe must be confirmed by what we do. Personal salvation must be expressed in ministry and mission in the world. We believe that Christian doctrine and Christian ethics are inseparable, that faith should inspire service. The integration of personal piety and social holiness has been a hallmark of our tradition. We affirm the biblical precept that "faith by itself, if it has no works, is dead" (James 2:17).

13. *Inclusive church.* The United Methodist Church is part of the church universal and includes people of all races and cultures, people with disabilities, people of all ages: children, youth, and adults. Therefore, "all people may attend its worship services, participate in its programs, receive the sacraments and become members in any local church in the connection."[12] We confess there have been times

when our attitudes toward one another betray our pronouncements about an inclusive church. To what extent do our congregations encourage and manifest a climate of welcome, a desire to learn from and share with one another?

14. *Connectional church.* Our local churches are part of a connectional system, which provides the structure for the way we carry out God's mission in the world. Connectionalism in the United Methodist tradition is multileveled, global in scope, and local in thrust. Our connectionalism is not merely a linking of one charge conference to another. Rather, it is a vital web of interactive relationships.

> We are connected by sharing a common tradition of faith, including our Doctrinal Standards and General Rules . . . ; by sharing together a constitutional polity, including a leadership of general superintendency; by sharing a common mission, which we seek to carry out by working together in and through conferences that reflect the inclusive and missional character of our fellowship; by sharing a common ethos that characterizes our distinctive way of doing things.[13]

15. *Sacraments.* The United Methodist Church recognizes, with many other Protestant churches, the two sacraments ordained by Christ: baptism and the Lord's Supper. "Sacraments ordained of Christ are not only badges or tokens of Christian men's profession, but rather they are certain signs of grace, and God's good will toward us, by which he doth work invisibly in us, and doth not only quicken, but also strengthen and confirm, our faith in him."[14]

Baptism celebrates God's grace bestowed on us and our initiation into Christ's holy church. Baptism marks the beginning of our new life in Christ and points us toward a life of Christian discipleship. (See pages 63–65 in Chapter Eight for more on baptism.)

Holy Communion—or the Lord's Supper or the Eucharist—celebrates God's love freely given to us in the life and sacrificial death of Jesus Christ. The Lord's Supper is God's invitation to commune and to be in fellowship with Christ. It also symbolizes our fellowship with other Christians. Holy Communion is the central act in our corporate worship experience. The United Methodist Church practices open Communion. Open means that all who "truly and

earnestly repent of [their] sins, and are in love and charity with
[their] neighbors, and intend to lead a new life, following the commandments of God,"[15] are invited to the table of the Lord.

The Task Before Us

The United Methodist Church has a long tradition of viewing
Christian belief and doctrine as a vital, living expression of faith. Yet,
we believe that the essence of Christian truth cannot be precisely
defined in statements about it. For that reason, our church would not
be considered a creedal church. Ancient creeds and confessions, as well
as modern affirmations, may be valid summaries of Christian truth, but
they do not represent our final authority. At best, they are attempts to
put into words what we believe and feel deeply about.

From the beginning, the early Methodists, United Brethren, and
Evangelicals looked to Christ as their ultimate authority. They searched
the Scripture. They looked to the collective wisdom of the pastors and
laypeople who made up their conferences. They turned to the hymns of
faith. Their emphasis was on new life in Christ and the Spirit's inner testimony, rather than on creedal assent.

The Methodists used Scripture, tradition, Christian experience, and
reason as guidelines. They read John Wesley's *Sermons and Notes* on
the New Testament. They studied the Articles of Religion prepared by
Wesley from similar Articles in the Church of England. The Evangelicals adopted a modified version of the Methodist Articles, and the
United Brethren had their Confession of Faith.

When The United Methodist Church was formed in 1968, the
Evangelical United Brethren Confession of Faith and the Methodist
Articles of Religion were both accepted as doctrinal standards for the
new church. Yet, we interpret neither of them in a legalistic or dogmatic
way. These standards, similar in perspective, are in our *Book of Discipline*.

So it is that we are called on to heed the Word and the will of God
supremely revealed in Christ and to give expression to the faith that
claims us. It is a humbling task and a high calling. We may not all speak
with one voice, but we are all constrained by one love. At times we will
be unable to live up to our profession; we will often fail, even in our
best efforts. But there is grace to redeem us and to sustain us on our
way. Thanks be to God!

CHAPTER EIGHT

MEMBERSHIP IN THE UNITED METHODIST CHURCH

he meaning of membership in The United Methodist Church is of vital concern to each of us. You may be a new Christian planning to unite with the church, or you may be transferring your membership from another denomination. If so, it is important that you understand the vows you make. You may already be a member of The United Methodist Church, perhaps for many years. A review of the commitments you once made may help you understand more fully the implications of your membership. Or, you may simply want to learn more about the church. I invite you to explore with me what membership in The United Methodist Church involves.

Baptism

Membership in The United Methodist Church begins with the sacrament of baptism. Baptism symbolizes the initiative God takes in bestowing on us grace and mercy and celebrates our complete dependence on God. Through the sacrament of baptism, we acknowledge God's gift of grace and are incorporated into the body of Christ, the church. We United Methodists affirm that baptism celebrates our covenant relationship with God.

Baptism has other implications. The apostle Paul spoke of being "baptized into Christ Jesus" (Romans 6:3). He may well have had in mind that we are partakers of the grace of Christ through baptism, as well as being initiated into the fellowship that had its origin in Christ. As far back as Old Testament times, as Gentiles converted into Judaism, baptism has been regarded as an entrance into the community of faith. Christian baptism signifies our initiation into the household of faith, Christ's holy church. (See *The United Methodist Hymnal,* page 33.)

We are baptized into Christ's universal church, not into a particular denomination or congregation. It is for this reason that we are baptized only once, and that our baptism is recognized by most other denominations. United Methodists, therefore, acknowledge the baptism of other Christian churches. People who transfer their membership from another denomination into our church are not rebaptized.

The United Methodist Church baptizes people of all ages. Baptism may be administered by sprinkling, pouring, or immersion. Infant baptism symbolizes in a unique way our utter dependence on God. It gives us one of our best insights into the true meaning of baptism at any age, because neither the infant nor we can, by our own works, earn God's grace. In a free act of outpouring love, God's grace is bestowed on us. God accepts us.

When infants or small children are baptized, their parents or sponsors praise God for this marvelous grace made known in Jesus Christ. They pledge, by teaching and example, to bring the children up in the Christian faith. They pledge to guide these children in ways that will enable them "to accept God's grace for themselves, to profess their faith openly, and to lead a Christian life."[1]

Then the congregation pledges to nurture these newly baptized members in the Christian faith:

> With God's help we will proclaim the good news
>   and live according to the example of Christ.
> We will surround *these persons*
>   with a community of love and forgiveness,
>   that *they* may grow in *their* service to others.
> We will pray for *them,*
>   that *they* may be true *disciples*
>   who *walk* in the way that leads to life.[2]

When youth and adults are baptized, the same utter dependence on God's grace is celebrated; but these people make a personal profession of faith at their baptism. In a single service they become baptized members of the church and then professing members. For all people, regardless of age, the primacy of grace, new life in Christ, entrance into the church, and Christian discipleship are at the heart of the sacrament of baptism.

Confirmation

The church offers various supportive ministries, caring relationships, and learning opportunities to help us live the Christian life symbolized by our baptism. This membership training is a lifelong process and is carried on through all the various activities of the church.

When those who became baptized members of the church as infants or as children grow to a time in their life when they are ready to claim the Christian faith as their own faith, they prepare for a service of confirmation where they will profess their faith. Preparation for confirmation examines what it means to be a professing member of the church. It focuses on the need for church members to know what it means to be in mission in all of life's relationships. It strengthens the resolve of those who are ready to profess their faith to be in ministry in the community and in the world. It enables them to discover ways to be engaged in helping others through Christian service and outreach.

Each pastor is responsible for providing preparation experiences for the youth and adults who are ready to profess their faith. In that confirmation service, baptized members of the church will declare their Christian faith and become professing members.

Profession of faith may occur several years after a child has been baptized, or it may be after the baptism of a youth or adult. The time of profession of faith has sometimes been referred to as a time when we join the church, or when we become members of the church. We need to keep in mind, however, that people are initiated into the fellowship of Christ's church at their baptism, when they become baptized members of the church. By making a profession of faith, baptized members make a personal, but public, profession of the faith that was professed by others (parents and the congregation) at their baptism. Those who commit themselves to Jesus Christ and profess faith in Christ as their Lord and Savior, and who are willing to assume the obligations of faithful membership in the church, become professing members of the congregation.

In the service of confirmation, water is used symbolically, and those being confirmed are asked to remember their baptism. Then the pastor, joined by others, lays hands on the confirmands as a sign of strengthening for living their profession by the power of the Holy Spirit.

The Vows We Make

The United Methodist Hymnal (1989 version, pages 33–39) summarizes the meaning of confirmation and lists the questions to which the one who wishes to become a professing member of the church is asked to respond:

> Through confirmation,
>   and through the reaffirmation of our faith,
>   we renew the covenant declared at our baptism,
>   acknowledge what God is doing for us,
>   and affirm our commitment to Christ's holy church....
>
> - Do you renounce the spiritual forces of wickedness,
>   reject the evil powers of this world,
>   and repent of your sin?
> - Do you accept the freedom and power God gives you
>   to resist evil, injustice, and oppression
>   in whatever forms they present themselves?
> - Do you confess Jesus Christ as your Savior,
>   put your whole trust in his grace,
>   and promise to serve him as your Lord,
>   in union with the church which Christ has opened
>   to people of all ages, nations, and races? ...
> - According to the grace given you,
>   will you remain *faithful members* of Christ's holy church
>   and serve as Christ's *representatives* in the world?[3]

Then, with the congregation, the confirmands profess the Christian faith as contained in the Scriptures of the Old and New Testaments using the Apostles' Creed. All of this constitutes the profession of faith and acceptance of the covenant relationship in terms of trust and basic practices.

When these questions have been answered in the affirmative, the pastor invites those being confirmed to "Remember your baptism and be thankful"[4] followed by the laying on of hands.

The pastor then asks questions that extend the vows to include statements of loyalty from the professing members of The United Methodist Church and to the congregation of which they are a part:

- As *members* of Christ's universal church,
  will you be loyal to The United Methodist Church,
  and do all in your power to strengthen its ministries?...
- As *members* of this congregation,
  will you faithfully participate in its ministries
  by your prayers, your presence,
  your gifts, and your service?[5]

After those who are making this profession of faith have answered, the congregation responds by renewing their own covenant, "that in everything God may be glorified through Jesus Christ."[6]

What do these vows mean? The earliest profession of faith found in the New Testament is that "Jesus Christ is Lord" (Philippians 2:11). The church from earliest times asked those committing themselves to life with the church to say no to evil and sin so that they are free to say yes to Jesus Christ in trust and service. The "renunciation and profession" section of the service invites this clear no and yes. This trust in Christ alone was the central orientation of Wesley and Asbury, Otterbein and Boehm, and Albright, who preached a gospel of new life in Christ. They knew what we must know: The world we live in is not neutral ground—there is strong resistance to living as Christ's representatives and to facing evil, injustice, and oppression. They also knew that there was a power that God gives to resist and to remain faithful with the church and in the world. When we profess the lordship of Christ, we commit ourselves to join with all Christians to help bring about transformed relationships and a world made new in Christ. The vision of Christ's kingdom, the reign of God in our midst, prompts us to pray, "Thy kingdom come, thy will be done."[7]

To live "according to the grace given to us" (Romans 12:6) affirms one of the most cherished themes of our heritage. We experience God's grace as undeserved love. Living in terms of grace involves making decisions on the basis of Christian hope and love. That is not easy for us to do. Sometimes our patience wears thin. We pray for greater sensitivity in trying to understand how Christian love can best be expressed in difficult and trying situations. It is what Wesley and others meant by growing in grace and being made perfect in love.

To remain faithful members of Christ's holy church throughout our lives challenges us with the vision of God's intended purpose for us and for the world. We pray that God will "grant us wisdom, grant us courage, for the facing of this hour."[8] The church as we know it may sometimes disappoint us, or we ourselves may be unfaithful. At times the voice of the church may be muted. Yet, within all the disappointment, God is faithful. God's love is constant and unfailing.

Our Commitment to Be in Ministry

It is possible to think of being loyal to the church and participating in its ministries only from an institutional point of view; that is, what takes place within the church. But any understanding of commitment that simply identifies prayer with church worship, presence with church attendance, gifts with church support, and service with church work is too restricted. As important as these expressions of our loyalty are, the faith we affirm moves beyond what takes place within the assembled congregation to what should occur when the congregation scatters in ministry. We will participate in the ministries of the church by upholding people for whom the church must care. We will participate in the ministries of the church by our commitment to those for whom Christ died. We will participate in the ministries of the church by expressing God's love for the world.

When we interpret our vows from the perspective of being in mission, as well as from what takes place within the gathered community of faith, we begin to understand how our commitments embrace all that we are, wherever we are, day by day.

Prayer

We will participate in the ministries of the church by our prayers. James Montgomery defines prayer as "the soul's sincere desire, unuttered or expressed;…the burden of a sigh;…the contrite sinner's voice;…the Christian's vital breath."[9] How would you define prayer?

For some time, I have thought of prayer as communication, communion, and community: communication as our expression of gratitude and thanksgiving, confession, and petition; communion as living day by day with the awareness of God's presence (praying without ceasing); and community as fellowship with others who lift heart and voice to the Eternal and who share their concerns for others in intercessory prayer.

We will pray that the work undertaken by our congregation will help accomplish those things we believe Christ would have us do; that the decision makers of the church, our community, and the world will be guided by the One who comes to bring life and hope and peace. We will pray for the pastor who shepherds us, for the teachers who instruct us, and for the friend who carries a heavy burden. We will pray for our own family and loved ones. We will pray for those who have wronged us.

We will pray for those who may never step inside a church, but who are broken in spirit; and for the sick and bereaved. We will take upon ourselves and bring before God the problems for which there are no easy solutions. We will pray that we ourselves, unworthy and limited as we are, can somehow be used to give heart and voice to the needs of others.

We will participate in the ministries of the church by our prayers, so that all we do within the church and community might express the will and compassion of Christ. When that begins to take place, the entire tone and atmosphere of a congregation begins to change.

Presence

We will participate in the ministries of the church by our presence. Someone asked an elderly man who had lost his hearing why he continued to come to church. His reply—"I want them to know which side I'm on"—emphasizes one of the reasons we participate in the ministries of the church by our presence: Our presence is a witness to our faith.

Worship attendance provides a meeting place—for the soul with God and for those who come together seeking spiritual guidance, comfort, and strength. Worship provides an atmosphere for reflection and self-evaluation. Worship helps us get our bearings. Worship surrounds us with our Christian heritage: the Scripture and hymns, ritual and the arts, those who have kept the faith and who have gone before us. Worship reminds us that we are part of a great company of faith.

We also participate in the ministries of the church by our presence throughout the week in our homes, at work, in recreation, at school, wherever we are. Our presence among others should speak of our commitment to Christ. God forbid that our presence on the job or after work should reveal one thing and our presence in the pew another. That is the real test of presence.

We will participate in the ministries of the church by being present when someone needs us: to give a listening ear or a sympathetic heart, to stand with, to walk beside when the storm beats hard. To send a letter or make a call, to give a gift—just to let others know we are with them, that is the church alive. Presence in the pew should reinforce our presence in the world.

Gifts

We will participate in the ministries of the church by our gifts. We will support the work and ministry of the church with our money; we will pledge, give systematically, tithe. We will give out of a thankful heart for all that God has given us.

We have opportunities through the church to lend our support to many worthy causes and institutions: hospitals, colleges, and homes; rehabilitation centers, counseling services; food and clothing distribution; scholarships and camping programs; evangelistic, educational, and social work; emergency relief. The list could be extended. Our World Service Fund, an apportioned benevolence, makes possible ministries that no individual or single congregation could do alone. Our pastoral ministries, community service, and property maintenance are all made possible because we participate in the ministries of the church by our gifts. Each congregation needs to examine its budget in terms of the amount that is designated to help others and the portion used for property and institutional maintenance.

Our gifts are not confined to financial contributions, however. We also have gifts of talents and abilities to share. People within and beyond our congregation need some gift that possibly only we can bring—the gift of counsel and companionship, the gift of love and laughter, the gift of conversation and song, the gift of something we have made with our own hands. The greatest gift we have to offer is the gift of ourselves. We can help someone through another day by participating in the ministries of the church with our gifts.

Service

We will participate in the ministries of the church by our service. Albert Schweitzer once said that the only people who will really be happy are those who have served. Teaching and preaching, serving on a committee, ushering, singing in the choir—all of these are needed services within the church. The number of people who volunteer their service in the various programs of the church is staggering.

I recall the retired farmer who is the handyman when something around the church building needs to be repaired, the primary public school teacher who works in vacation Bible school, the youth who have a car wash to raise money for tornado victims, the woman who gives her flowers to the sick, the woman who spends long hours working in the church kitchen, and the child who makes a get-well card for a neighbor in the hospital.

Faith and service do indeed go hand in hand. The New Testament calls us to be a servant people, to give ourselves for others. We participate in the ministries of the church by doing what we believe Christ would have us do in the community. We visit the sick and those in our institutional care facilities. We explore ways that enable older adults to remain in their own homes as long as possible. We work for justice and equity across racial lines. We give expression to our Christian citizenship by becoming knowledgeable about, and engaged in, social and political issues. We sponsor food and clothing collections for the needy. There is no end to the kinds of activities in which we, the servant people of God, can invest our time and abilities.

Renewed Confirmation

Yes, we will be loyal to The United Methodist Church and participate in its ministries with our prayers, our presence, our gifts, and our service. It may all begin within the church, within the context of a worship service, a Sunday school class, or a fellowship group. It may be nurtured there, but it does not remain there. It moves out into the community and world about us to the world that God loves and to which Christ comes as Savior. Let us rejoice that the church of Jesus Christ can become the people through whom God's redemptive love is made real to a needy world.

The confirmation of our faith through these vows celebrates a high calling. Although we can date the time and place of our service of confirmation, we recognize that confirmation is an ongoing commitment. It is not something we can simply put behind us when the event is over.

During important events in our lives, we need to confirm our faith again. Significant events such as birth, marriage, death, separation, moving, assuming a new job, unemployment, retirement—all of these provide opportunities to remember our baptism and to renew the commitments we made when we professed our faith, knelt at the altar of the church, and claimed our covenant in Christ.

CHAPTER NINE

THE LAITY IN MINISTRY

=)«(O)»=

ook over the congregation on a Sunday morning. Most of those sitting around you are probably ordinary people like you. Among them are friends and neighbors who are happy, lonely, hopeful, tempted, confident, fearful. They represent a mighty force for doing the work of God in the world. Think of the influence each of you in your congregation has—or could have—as you leave the sanctuary and go to your home, the classroom, the office, the field, wherever your place of work is, or wherever your life takes you. The ministry of the people in the pew is what we are concerned with here.

Jesus himself looked to just such people to bear witness to the good news of God's love. The common, ordinary people of Jesus' day were entrusted with the gospel to be "the salt of the earth" and "the light of the world" (Matthew 5:13-14). They were to live by the Sermon on the Mount and go into the world with the vision of God's kingdom. Among Jesus' first disciples were fishermen and a tax collector. The twelve disciples who were called were Jewish laity. The term *laity* comes from the Greek word *laos*, which means "the people of God." That includes all of us.

The term *ministry* may suggest to you something only pastors do, some kind of service performed by people with special training, or something that is done within the church. But ministry is not restricted to these kinds of activities. Ministry includes the witness and the helping and caring kinds of service we all do in carrying out our Christian discipleship as the servant people of God.

Our One Call

The New Testament ascribes high attributes to the Christians of the early church. They are called by God; they are God's own people, a chosen race, a royal priesthood. I suspect most of them were not too different from us.

The apostle Paul reminds us that we all share a common call: "There is one body and one Spirit, just as you were called to the one hope of your calling, one Lord, one faith, one baptism, one God and Father of all, who is above all and through all and in all" (Ephesians 4:4-6). Those words were written to the Christians in the church at Ephesus, to the "faithful in Christ Jesus" (Ephesians 1:1). What a motley group they must have been.

The author of First Peter addressed his letter to the Christians in exile and reminded them that they were indeed the people of God:

> You are a chosen race, a royal priesthood, a holy nation, God's own people, in order that you may proclaim the mighty acts of {the One] who called you out of darkness into...light.
>> Once you were not a people,
>> but now you are God's people;
>> once you had not received mercy,
>> but now you have received mercy.   (1 Peter 2:9-10)

Our *Book of Discipline* reiterates these biblical themes by emphasizing the call of all Christians to be in ministry: "All Christians are called to minister wherever Christ would have them serve and witness in deeds and words that heal and free."[1] Yes, each one of us affirms, "A charge to keep I have, a God to glorify."[2]

Our ministry is inspired by Jesus Christ, who "came not to be served but to serve" (Matthew 20:28). Our ministry is a shared one, with pastors and laity working together, mutually encouraging and supporting one another in a common task. Our functions vary, but our call to obedience is the same.

The Letter to the Ephesians defines the equipping role of church leaders: Christ's gifts are "that some would be apostles, some prophets, some evangelists, some pastors and teachers, to equip the saints for the work of ministry, for building up the body of Christ" (Ephesians 4:11-12).

Paul's emphasis is on strengthening and equipping the people of God for ministry as a witnessing community of faith.

Paul's analogy of the church as the body of Christ reinforces our need for one another: "For as in one body we have many members, and not all the members have the same function, so we, who are many, are one body in Christ, and individually we are members one of another" (Romans 12:4-6).

Ministry as Daily Discipleship

Ministry is being where we believe Christ would have us be—indeed, being where Christ is present. Ministry is doing what we believe Christ would have us do. Ministry is living day by day the life of Christian discipleship. Ministry may not involve that which is spectacular. It may not represent some heroic action. Usually no trumpets are sounded.

I recall a neighbor who, as she grew older, found it increasingly difficult to get around. No longer able to attend church because of a disability, she still found a way to help others. Neighbors and friends brought bags of leftover pieces of fabric from sewing projects to her. She sorted, ironed, cut, and matched quilt pieces, and spent day after day sewing and putting together quilts and comforters. She gave them to the church to distribute to the needy and to mission projects at home and abroad. Her ministry was an example of John Wesley's admonition to show "desire of salvation...by doing good of every possible sort, and as far as possible, to all."[3]

At times we seem to be thrust into ministry. Sometimes, for conscience sake, we must challenge existing policies and stand alone. Sometimes all we can do is stand beside a friend or family member through a difficult time. In such cases, our ministry seems to be decided for us. There are no easy solutions, for instance, when a teenager is on drugs, a marriage fails, or an aging parent has deteriorated to the point of needing constant care. The place of ministry in such cases is in the midst of the problem. It involves lending what stability and hope we can, seeking God's grace and guidance in making the best possible decisions under trying circumstances, and being present with the one who needs us.

Some Guidelines for Ministry

We are always in the learning stage when it comes to knowing how we can most effectively carry out our ministry as disciples of Christ. We need to think of ministry in terms of our daily response to God with those whom we have an opportunity to serve in the spirit of Christ. It involves a Christian witness, advocacy and action, and a Christian presence.

Here are ten guidelines for our daily ministry that, in my experience, hold true:

1. Realize that you are not alone. God's grace will sustain you.

2. Be sensitive to the needs of others. Try to put yourself in their place. How might you feel if you were in their situation? What might you do to respond to their need? What might the church do? Some needs require combined action.

3. Consider yourself on call in terms of those who need you. Make yourself available. At the same time, don't wait to be asked. Many people who most desperately need friendship and help are hesitant to make their needs known.

4. Recognize that you do not have all the answers. You may not be able to change the situation at hand, but you have compassion and understanding to share. You can point to the One who makes all things new. You may be conscious of your own needs and inadequacies in trying to minister to others. If you are conscious of your own need for healing and wholeness, you can offer yourself, in the words of Henri Nouwen, as a "wounded healer."

5. As you minister with and to others, be willing to deal with the unexpected. Remain flexible. There may well be surprises no one can predict. The good Samaritan of Jesus' parable had not planned to come upon a fellow traveler who had been beaten and robbed. His schedule was interrupted because someone needed him. Those who had passed by on the other side kept their appointments.

6. Be willing to accept failure. Everything may not turn out just the way you want it to. You will need to learn to live with an awareness of the incomplete and the unfinished.

7. Be willing to accept people as they are, with all their failures and shortcomings. That is the way God accepts us.

8. Be willing to tackle one small part of a big problem, realizing that you may not be able to transform the entire situation. You may not be able to feed an entire population of starving people, but you can feed one child.

9. Know that ministry involves both giving and receiving. How often I have tried to lend support to someone facing a crisis only to find that I came away strengthened by the one I had come to help. In ministering, I was ministered to.

10. Keep your eyes fixed on Christ. Mother Teresa of Calcutta asked that people pray for her so that she would not lose sight of Christ, even while ministering to the poor. That is the secret of sharing our gifts and our lives with others.

Ways We Find and Provide Support

Many people feel alone on their Christian journey. You may have felt that way at one time or another. People such as these face problems of which most of us are unaware. Their patience and faith are put to the test. Sometimes these people reach the breaking point.

All of us need support, encouragement, and affirmation as we seek to live out our lives of Christian discipleship. We need to know that there is someone to whom we can turn, someone with whom we can talk things over, someone who understands. You and I can be that kind of person to someone else. Without doubt, the tasks that laypeople handle inside the church are important. But the most significant ministry of laypeople is to be disciples in their families, in their communities, and in the places where they work and play. Small groups within the ministry of the church can help equip laypeople to live as disciples who witness to their personal faith in the world where they live, helping others to feel God's love.

Our relationship with God and with the people of God is of primary importance in finding the strength and support we need for our ministry. We turn to God, not because we have nowhere else to turn, but because God is our source of strength and hope. Prayer and worship and Bible reading are sustaining influences in our lives.

A number of us wondered how a man whose wife had died, whose son had committed suicide, and whose daughter had died of leukemia was able to hold up and to carry on. Through each shattering experience, he seemed to be a source of strength for others in his family. He said his secret was that he could not do it on his own. The Christ of faith came to him as a ministering presence. His friends, neighbors, and pastor came through each experience with him. Even though he was unaware of it, his own faith was a Christian witness and a real ministry to others.

We support one another for ministry and in ministry by our presence, encouragement, faith, and prayer. It is a matter of assuring people they are not alone. Many times this is done on a one-on-one basis. At other times, some kind of intentional, organized effort is needed.

A Ministry Without Limits

Since our ministry is a manifestation of our Christian discipleship, it has no limits. We go where we believe Christian duty calls us to go, and we do what we believe Christian conscience tells us to do. Ministry may occur both within the church and in the world about us. We have within The United Methodist Church thousands of volunteer officers and teachers, lay leaders and lay speakers, people who are giving their time and talent serving on committees, singing in choirs, ushering, and the like. They lead study groups, sponsor retreats, and head up service projects. They visit in homes, hospitals, nursing care facilities, and jails. They cooperate with other church and civic groups in addressing the problems and needs of the community. They represent one of the largest groups of volunteers to be found anywhere in the world.

Ministry knows no age limits. How often have you thought of the ministry of little children? The love and trust of a little child is often the healing touch we need. A children's choir presents a benefit concert to raise money for starving children. A Sunday school class makes tray favors for a local nursing home. Yes, children also are part of the *laos,* the people of God.

A high school boy adopts a grandparent, makes occasional visits, and runs errands. The youth group has a car wash to raise money for flood victims. Youth learn about the hazards of drugs and encourage others to kick the habit. They, too, are part of the *laos* in ministry.

A high school teacher who had worked with young people over the years suffered a severe stroke. Partially paralyzed, his speech affected, and confined to a wheelchair, he wondered what he could do now. His possibilities for ministry seemed limited. But he said, "There is one thing I can and will do. I will pray for them." The bond between the teacher and his former students was greatly strengthened when they knew of his love and concern for them. One ministered to the other.

A young mother organizes a telephone reassurance ministry to ensure that people who are limited in their ability to leave home are all right. A coach teaches a Sunday school class. A secretary leads a prayer retreat. Yes, we are all part of the *laos,* called to "serve and witness in deeds and words that heal and free."[4]

Ministry knows no limits between the personal and the social dimensions of our faith. A vital piety and social responsibility must always be held together. That was the conviction of our early founders, who were the heralds of personal salvation and social reform. Today, many churches have opened food pantries and clothes closets for those in need. Christians have opened their church buildings to those who need shelter or refuge. Christians respond with loving care to the victims of floods, tornadoes, and hurricanes. Christians everywhere are involved in Meals on Wheels and in daycare for mothers who must work. Christians give their time and money to support the work of many community service organizations.

Christians not only respond to needs but also work to change the circumstances that create crime, poverty, and despair. Changing the basic causes of societal problems is a dimension of our ministry that must receive more and more attention. How can we become proactive, not just reactive, in addressing human issues? Response to human need is crucial; yet, we recognize our responsibility in trying to head off some of the causes that create the need.

Our ministry must often take on tough issues. It calls for keeping our priorities straight. Amos, the shepherd, reminded his people that their ceremonies and sacrifices were hollow without attention to the oppressed, the poor, and the needy: "I hate, I despise your festivals, and I take no delight in your solemn assemblies.... Take away from me the noise of your songs; I will not listen to the melody of your harps. But let justice roll down like waters, and righteousness like an ever-flowing stream" (Amos 5:21-24).

The Social Creed of our church provides a working base for our ministry. It can help us, in our day, keep our minds and hearts fixed on important issues.

Our Social Creed

We believe in God, Creator of the world; and in Jesus Christ, the Redeemer of creation. We believe in the Holy Spirit, through whom we acknowledge God's gifts, and we repent of our sin in misusing these gifts to idolatrous ends.

We affirm the natural world as God's handiwork and dedicate ourselves to its preservation, enhancement, and faithful use by humankind.

We joyfully receive for ourselves and others the blessings of community, sexuality, marriage, and the family.

We commit ourselves to the rights of men, women, children, youth, young adults, the aging, and people with disabilities; to improvement of the quality of life; and to the rights and dignity of racial, ethnic, and religious minorities.

We believe in the right and duty of persons to work for the glory of God and the good of themselves and others and in the protection of their welfare in so doing; in the rights to property as a trust from God, collective bargaining, and responsible consumption; and in the elimination of economic and social distress.

We dedicate ourselves to peace throughout the world, to the rule of justice and law among nations, and to individual freedom for all people of the world.

We believe in the present and final triumph of God's Word in human affairs and gladly accept our commission to manifest the life of the gospel in the world. Amen.[5]

Our Summons to Evangelism

Our ministry as the people of God involves witness as well as service-witness by word and deed. Our church was born in evangelism. John Wesley told those who worked in ministry, "You have nothing to do but to save souls."[6] And Charles Wesley sang, "I set my seal that Jesus is true... O let me commend my Saviour to you."[7]

We dare not restrict evangelism to our witness by deeds alone. It is true that we are called on to exemplify the mind and spirit of Christ by how we live and what we do. Often, our actions do speak louder than our words. At the same time, we have a story to tell. Had someone not told the marvelous story that God has met our deepest needs and highest hopes in Jesus Christ, we might never have begun our journey of faith. Evangelism is reaching out to others, telling the gospel story, and helping them begin, or continue, their pilgrimage with Christ. It is the story of how God in Christ saves us from a life of self-centeredness, sin, and despair; saves us within our helpless and confused condition; and saves us to a new life in the Spirit wherein all things become new.

There is no more important task facing The United Methodist Church today. The number of churches that receive no new members on profession of faith throughout an entire year is appalling. How many people united with your congregation this past year on profession of faith? Such lay evangelists as Harry Denman reminded the church that we must never forget our imperative of telling others about Jesus Christ.

How do we bear witness to Jesus Christ? How do we go about carrying out this kind of ministry as the people of God? These guidelines may help:

1. Discover what your congregation is doing in its evangelistic outreach. Discuss it with your pastor and with other laypeople. Assume your own responsibility as a Christian witness.

2. Recognize that you are not alone as you tell the gospel to others. Rely on the presence of the Holy Spirit.

3. Remember, you have the *evangel* (good news) to share the story of Jesus Christ and the new quality of life in which all may share, a life of love and service in the world and for the world. You have your own faith journey to draw on. You can tell others what Christ means to you.

4. Relate to others out of genuine love, interest, and concern. Go as a friend, be a friend, leave and remain as a friend.

5. Respect the integrity and freedom of others. Avoid placing others in embarrassing positions. Avoid psychological pressure and the use of religious clichés.

6. Let the telling of the gospel message be as natural as possible. Do not hesitate to tell about your own ups and downs on your Christian journey. Remember, however, that your focus is on new life in Christ.

7. Be a good listener; don't preach. Above all, let it be known that you are also on your own journey of faith, that conversion and discipleship involve a dynamic process of growth. Invite others to walk with Christ by faith along with you.

8. Where appropriate, follow up your visit. Be supportive. Inform your pastor of your conversation where a call needs to be made.

9. If people decide to unite with the church, continue to lend your encouragement and support as they begin their own ministry and outreach.

10. Keep before your congregation the opportunities to minister not only to the physical and social needs of people but also to their spiritual needs.

Albert Outler said:

> Give us a church whose members believe and understand the gospel of God's healing love of Christ to hurting men and women. Give us a church that speaks and acts in consonance with its faith—not only to reconcile the world but to turn it upside down! Give us a church of Spirit-filled people in whose fellowship life speaks to life, love to love, and faith and trust respond to God's grace. And we shall have a church whose witness in the world will not fail and whose service to the world will transform it.[8]

That is the kind of church God can give us as our laity and pastors lay claim to, and are possessed by, the urgency of the gospel. God help us to make it our own.

CHAPTER TEN

THE CONGREGATION IN MISSION

hose of us who love the church know that at its best the church can elicit feelings of joy, generosity, and comfort. Yet, there are times when the church can also produce feelings of frustration and confusion. Have you experienced this paradox of the reality of the church? Lifeless is the church that has lost its vision and compassion. Vibrant is the church whose message is "Emmanuel...God is with us!"

How does the church shape its ministry so that Christ becomes its way, its truth, and its life (John 14:6)? Some churches focus their attention inward on themselves. They are concerned with the prosperity of their building and with having all that they need to be comfortable. They use their money to pay the preacher, to be sure that the sanctuary is heated and cooled, and to decorate with fancy cushions and furniture so that those who come to their church will be encouraged to return. Other congregations see beyond themselves to the needs of the community and world in which they live. Like their Lord, they are willing to give their lives for the sake of others; they are willing to become agents of change and reconciliation.

Jesus' ministry of teaching, preaching, and healing sets the pattern for the church. The purpose of the church can be none other than to continue the ministry Jesus began. That was the conviction of the first disciples at Pentecost, who extended the work of their crucified Lord and rejoiced in the assurance that Christ was still with them to guide and sustain them. That is also our assurance as The United Methodist Church.

We are concerned with how we continue and provide for the ministry to which Christ calls us, how we carry out the mission of the church. Each congregation is summoned to mission through its witness by word and deed.

> We are called together for worship and fellowship and for the upbuilding of the Christian community. We advocate and work for the unity of the Christian church. We call all persons into discipleship under the Lordship of Jesus Christ.

> As servants of Christ we are sent into the world to engage in the struggle for justice and reconciliation. We seek to reveal the love of God for men, women, and children of all ethnic, racial, cultural, and national backgrounds and to demonstrate the healing power of the gospel with those who suffer.[1]

It is primarily at the local level that the church moves out to encounter the community and world. What Jesus said concerning the individual is also true of the church: If we try to save our life, we will lose it; but if we lose our life for the sake of Christ and the gospel, we will save it (Mark 8:35). The church finds its real purpose and reason for being in a life of servanthood.

Our Church Community

The local church is a "community of true believers under the Lordship of Christ." It is a "redemptive fellowship." It exists for "the maintenance of worship, the edification of believers, and the redemption of the world."[2]

Local churches are to be found in all shapes and sizes, in cities, villages, and the open country. The United Methodist Church embraces most ethnic cultures and many of the world languages. We celebrate our pluralistic heritage, the richness of our ethnic cultures, and the inclusiveness of the Christian community that makes us brothers and sisters in Christ.

> Today all ethnic minority groups bring distinctive and valued gifts to our whole church. Some bring new hymns and new forms of worship. Some share an evangelistic zeal and a passionate commitment to social justice. Some teach us to be quiet, to be open and receptive to the Holy Spirit's work. All help us learn to live as Christians in an intercultural world.[3]

Called to witness and mission in our world, every local church is asked to give prayer, study, and financial support for developing and strengthening ethnic minority local churches for witness and mission. The whole church is called on to join with our ethnic congregations in extending their ministry.

Here are ways in which the congregation as a community of believers and as a redemptive fellowship carries out the mission of the church.

1. *The congregation is a worshiping community.* We believe that worship should occupy a central place in the life of every Christian. Our lives are renewed and sustained through prayer, the reading of the Scripture, through the sacraments, by music and preaching, and in fellowship with other Christians. We acknowledge the need of our spiritual formation growing "to the measure of the full stature of Christ" (Ephesians 4:13).

   We encourage both individual and corporate worship. Devotional guides, spiritual formation events, Bible study, and prayer retreats all contribute to the life of the spirit.

2. *The congregation is a teaching and learning community.* The Sunday school, the United Methodist Women, the United Methodist Men, and groups of different age levels provide opportunities for study, reflection, and action. Basic biblical and theological foundations for Christian education in The United Methodist Church are found in *Foundations: Shaping the Ministry of Christian Education in Your Congregation.* This statement of purpose is found in that book:

   > Through Christian education we invite people and communities of faith to be transformed as they are inspired and challenged to
   > - Know and experience God through Jesus Christ,
   > - Claim and live God's promises, and
   > - Grow and serve as Christian disciples.[4]

3. *The congregation is a witnessing community.* We believe that a biblical and theological understanding of evangelism embraces the personal, corporate, and social dimensions of the gospel—that individuals, groups, and systems need to come under the transforming and redemptive love of Christ. Each congregation is called on to assist individual Christians in witnessing to their faith by word and deed, to invite others to faith in Christ, and to sustain them on their Christian pilgrimage.

It is our responsibility and privilege to invite and receive people into the fellowship and membership of the church, to nurture them in the faith, and to maintain a lively interest in their Christian growth and faithfulness to the gospel and to the church.

4. *The congregation is a sharing community.* We are called on to give our financial resources, our time, and our talents to extend Christ's work and will in the world. Out of a sense of the stewardship of all life, we affirm that our gifts and resources are to be viewed and used as a trust from God. Our gifts and service meet the needs of individuals and families in our communities and around the world. The stewardship program of our local church supports World Service ministries and agencies, humanitarian and benevolent causes, current expenses, and the capital needs of the congregation.

5. *The congregation is a serving community.* As Christ's life was given for others, so we heed the words "just as you did it to one of the least of these...you did it to me" (Matthew 25:40). We confess that we are Christ's hands in the world, and we gladly offer ourselves for service and ministry. Each congregation is called on to identify the people and places of need, to design ways that address those needs, and to support those who are engaged in ministry.

Worship, teaching and learning, witnessing, sharing, and serving represent the major thrusts of most congregations in carrying out the mission of the church.

The Primary Task of the Congregation

The General Board of Discipleship has identified four essential functions of the local church, known as the primary task of the congregation. They represent ways in which the church can become a vital force in carrying out its mission. They also portray the kinds of concern and the spirit that should permeate each of our efforts. Consider ways in which your own congregation bears the mark of these emphases.

1. *Receiving*—reaching out to accept and receive people as they are. The congregation should manifest a spirit of friendliness, openness, and acceptance. It should be the kind of fellowship that welcomes those who enter the church. But more than that, the

congregation should reach out to others, invite them to take part, support them as friends. The receiving, reaching, and accepting function of the congregation knows no boundaries of race, culture, or human condition. It is a ministry that must be translated into individual responsibility.

Our reaching out to others and accepting them as they are is inspired by the example of Jesus and by the knowledge that this is the way God deals with each of us. God reaches out with boundless love to receive us and to point us toward a life of new possibilities. Thus, we are to reach out to and accept others with all their limitations and faults, all their strengths and graces. We are able to bear, and to bear with, all the disappointment, tragedy, and pain in the lives of others, without despair and bitterness, because we ourselves have known the mercy of a forgiving and loving God.

2. *Relating*—helping people relate their lives to God. Through the various major thrusts of the church, whether it be through worship or a Sunday school class or a service project, one of our primary concerns is that individuals come into, or be strengthened in, a relationship with God. While we speak of helping others relate their lives to God, we admit that this is also our need. Regardless of how long we have been on the Christian journey, we are always aware that we need a closer walk with the One who is our life and hope. Every time we sing, "O for a closer walk with God,"[5] we make that our hope and prayer. What a privilege we have as individuals and as a church to help one another on this journey.

3. *Strengthening*—sustaining and supporting Christians as disciples. It was said of the early Christians, "See how they love one another." That was the distinctive mark of the Christian fellowship. One of the most important contributions of a congregation is its supportive fellowship. A Christian fellowship is more than a gathering of congenial, like-minded people. It represents a relationship in which Christ is central.

Within a Christian fellowship one feels accepted and loved. It is within the fellowship that genuine care and concern are expressed. It is there that one finds understanding and the opportunity for growth. All the various activities of the church should support and encourage us on our Christian pilgrimage. Several studies over the years have shown that many people are attracted to and remain in the Sunday school, or another small group, because of the fellowship they find there. It is indicative both of our need and of the strengthening influence of the Christian fellowship.

4. *Sending*—giving encouragement and support to the faithful for ministry in the communities where they live and work. There is a sense in which we send out and support one another in ministry. At the same time, we know that it is God who sends us into our communities to help make them more loving and just. It is Christ who commands us to go into the world and make disciples. It is a primary task of the congregation not only to identify areas of ministry in the community and world but to affirm and encourage those who are living out their lives in obedience to the gospel.

On November 14, 1940, the beautiful Coventry Cathedral in England was reduced to ruins in an air raid. Today, next to the new cathedral stands the gutted remains of the old church with the open sky above. A cross made from some charred timbers rises above an altar with the inscription "Father Forgive." Through the centuries the cathedral had a series of guild chapels dating back to the industrial guilds of medieval times. Now, in the place of those chapels are stations marked with plaques called Hallowing Places. The prayers at the Hallowing Places are to be carried back into daily life and used frequently. The Hallowing Places remind us of what it means to be sent out as disciples to make our communities and world more loving and just.

> IN INDUSTRY: God be in my hands and in my making.
> IN THE ARTS: God be in my senses and in my creating.
> IN THE HOME: God be in my heart and in my loving.
> IN COMMERCE: God be at my desk and in my trading.
> IN HEALING: God be in my skill and in my touching.
> IN GOVERNMENT: God be in my plans and in my deciding.
> IN EDUCATION: God be in my mind and in my growing.
> IN RECREATION: God be in my limbs and in my leisure.[6]

What a ministry and mission we have as a church and as disciples of Christ. It calls for vision, for repentance, and for renewed faith. To think that we have been entrusted with the gospel for such a day as this is a high calling and an urgent task.

What of the Future?

We have examined thus far our United Methodist heritage and our call to live as Christian disciples today. But what of the future? The makeup of our family units continues to change. People are increasingly living and working on a global basis. Every aspect of our lives is affected by technological advances. More and more people are on the move. Communication technology provides instant information. An increasing number of people seek to control their own destiny. Military technology and production continue to drain the energies and economies of many of the nations of the world. These realities continue to be true, and our calling for the future is to see a vision of what is possible with the reconciling and restoring love of God.

As we look to the future, we pray for wisdom and humility, for grace sufficient for the tasks that await us. We pray for understanding and tolerance, for the unity of the church, that we may be one. We pray that God will strengthen the witness and ministry of the church, beginning with each of us.

CHAPTER ELEVEN

The Local Church and Its Connections

he United Methodist Church is a connectional church. That is to say, each congregation is linked to, or is connected with, all other churches throughout the entire organization. The local church is a crucial link in our connectional system. It is not simply one link in the chain; it is the fundamental link.

The connectional system of the church is much like the apostle Paul's analogy of the church as the body of Christ. The system has many parts, each distinct from the other, yet all interdependent and connected. Indeed, the well-being of the whole system depends on the health of each part.

The connectedness of one congregation to the other has its origin in the days of Wesley, Otterbein, Boehm, and Albright. No congregation, or part of the church, can look only to itself. We look to the well-being of the whole church and give thanks for our unity in Christ.

Servant Ministry and Servant Leadership

All Christians are called by their baptism to a ministry of servant-hood in the world.

Very early in its history, the church came to understand that all of its members were commissioned in baptism to ministries of love, justice, and service within local congregations and the larger communities in which they lived; all who follow Jesus have a share in the ministry of Jesus, who came not to be served, but to serve. There is thus a general ministry of all baptized Christians.[1]

The church also recognizes that within the people of God some are called to an ordained ministry, either as a deacon or as an elder.

1. The *deacon* is ordained to lead the church in the servanthood that every Christian is called to through baptism. Deacons, called by God, ordained by a bishop, and members in full connection with an annual conference, embody and model the relationship between worship in the congregation and service to God's people in the world.

   The word *deacon* comes from the Greek root *diakonos,* which means servant. Deacons are ordained to the ministries of Word and Service. Deacons teach and proclaim the Word, participate in worship leadership, assist elders in the administration of the sacraments, conduct weddings and funerals, and lead the congregation in servant ministry in the world.

   Deacons may serve the church either as an appointed staff member of a local church or denominational agency or through an appointment outside the local church that takes the servant ministry of the church into the world.

2. The *elder* is ordained to lead the church in Service, Word, Sacrament, and Order. Elders are called by God, ordained by a bishop, and members in full connection with an annual conference. They preach and teach the Word of God, administer the sacraments of baptism and Holy Communion, and order the life of the church for mission and ministry.

   Elders fulfill the ministry of the *presbyteros,* whose historical role in the church was to assist the bishop with the celebration of the sacraments and with the guidance and care for the gathered communities of faith. This early task of guidance and prayer is carried out by the elder as he or she orders the life of the congregation and participates in the services of weddings, funerals, and other celebrations of important events among the members of the congregation.

Elders are itinerant ministers who serve as appointed by the bishop. The work of the elder is most often done in a local congregation, but they sometimes serve in extension ministries beyond the local church.

It is also important to remember that there are laypeople who are called to serve in ministry through an annual conference. A *local pastor,* although not ordained, may be licensed and then appointed by a bishop to perform the duties of a pastor in a specific local church.

Local Church Organization

Each local congregation of The United Methodist Church is charged with the responsibility for organizing so that the primary task of the church—reaching out and receiving people, helping people to commit their lives to a relationship with God, providing opportunities for strengthening that relationship and growing in spiritual formation, and supporting them as they are sent forth into the world to live as faithful disciples—can be accomplished in the area where the local church is found. The organization developed by the local congregation must enable the congregation to fulfill six basic responsibilities:

1. Planning and implementing a program of nurture, outreach, and witness for persons and families within and without the congregation;
2. Providing for effective pastoral and lay leadership;
3. Providing for financial support, physical facilities, and the legal obligations of the church;
4. Utilizing the appropriate relationships and resources of the district and annual conference;
5. Providing for the proper creation, maintenance, and disposition of documentary record material of the local church; and
6. Seeking inclusiveness in all aspects of its life.[2]

How is your congregation organized?

Within each pastoral charge is a charge conference, which meets at least annually. The charge conference is the connecting link between the local church and the general church. Its primary responsibility is to review and evaluate the total mission and ministry of the church, receive reports, and adopt objectives and goals recommended by the church council. The district superintendent, or a designated elder, presides over the charge conference.

District Organization

Each local church is part of a district. Each district covers a geographic area and may include from fifty to ninety or more churches. In what district is your church located? A district superintendent is an elder appointed by the bishop to oversee the ministry of the pastors and that of each church in the district. Who is the superintendent of your district?

A district superintendent is appointed by the bishop of the annual conference where the district is located. A district superintendent usually serves for up to six years, but that time can be extended to up to eight years if the bishop makes that appointment in consultation with the cabinet and with the district committee on superintendency. No superintendent may be appointed for more than eight years in any consecutive eleven years, and no elder can serve as a district superintendent for more than twelve years. A district conference shall be held if directed by the annual conference, or it may be called by the district superintendent.

The Annual Conference

The annual conference, comprising several districts, is the fundamental United Methodist structure beyond the congregation. What is the name of your annual conference? The yearly meetings of the annual conferences in the United States are attended by lay members and clergy. In addition, there are are several central conferences located outside the United States, including Africa, Europe, and the Philippines.

The bishop of the area presides over the annual conferences. More than one annual conference may be located within an episcopal area. The annual conference, which is the basic body of the church, reviews the work of the previous year and plans programs and ministries for the coming year, in keeping with the *Discipline* and the General Rules of the church. It is at the annual conference that the bishop fixes the pastoral appointments of the clergy, who are appointed for one year at a time.

The Jurisdictional Conference

A jurisdiction is a geographic region made up of several conferences. The United States has five jurisdictions: Northeastern, Southeastern, North Central, South Central, and Western.

The jurisdictional conferences meet every four years and are made up of an equal number of laypeople and clergy. The conferences are presided over by the bishops of the jurisdictions, or by a bishop from another jurisdiction or a central conference. The primary functions of a jurisdictional conference are to promote the evangelistic, educational, missionary, and benevolent interests of the church; elect elders as bishops and provide for their support as determined by the General Conference; select jurisdictional representatives to the general boards of the church; and establish the boundaries of their annual conferences.

Bishops are assigned to their episcopal areas for a four-year term at this conference. Ordinarily, a bishop may not serve in the same episcopal area for more than eight years. However, a third quadrennium may be recommended if it is considered to be in the best interest of the jurisdiction by a two-thirds vote of the jurisdictional committee on episcopacy and the jurisdictional conference. Who is the bishop of your episcopal area?

The General Conference

The General Conference alone speaks for The United Methodist Church as a whole. It is the lawmaking body of our church. The General Conference meets every four years and is made up of an equal number of lay and clergy delegates representing each of the annual conferences and central conferences.

The General Conference initiates and directs all connectional enterprises of the church. It provides boards and agencies to assist in the work of the church. It governs the matters of church membership and defines the responsibilities of the other conferences of the connectional system. It determines the qualifications, nature, and function of the ordained ministry. It gives major direction to the evangelistic and missional outreach of the church.

The Council of Bishops

The United Methodist Church has an episcopal form of government. Bishops are appointed to give general oversight and spiritual leadership to the church and are called to be the shepherds of the people. The Council of Bishops is composed of all the bishops of the church. The

Council meets to promote the temporal and spiritual interests of the entire church and to carry into effect the rules, regulations, and responsibilities prescribed by the General Conference.

The Judicial Council

The United Methodist Church is similar to the federal government, in that it has three branches: the executive (the Council of Bishops), the legislative (the General Conference), and the judicial (the Judicial Council). The Judicial Council is the Supreme Court of our denomination. It determines the constitutionality of General Conference actions and the legality of other matters referred to it.

The General Council on Finance and Administration

The General Council on Finance and Administration is accountable to United Methodists through the General Conference in all matters relating to the receiving, disbursing, and reporting of funds contributed for the support of national and worldwide ministries.

Program-Related Agencies

The United Methodist Church has four program boards and four commissions. Annual conferences relate to the objectives and responsibilities of the general agencies through designated leaders, committees, or boards.

Boards

The General Board of Church and Society relates the Christian gospel to the whole of life, focuses attention on the major issues of the day, and shows members of the church and society that God's reconciliation involves personal, social, and civic righteousness. It seeks the implementation of the Social Principles of our church in the formation and administration of public policy.

The General Board of Discipleship provides resources and services to help local churches and conferences make disciples of Jesus Christ. This board helps local congregations carry out the primary task and provides resources to support growth in Christian discipleship.

The General Board of Global Ministries is the agency that facilitates world and national missions, enhances the spiritual empowerment and world ministry of women, and is engaged in relief work and health and welfare ministries. It works for the unity of Christ's church. It supports missionaries and provides opportunities for many volunteers.

The General Board of Higher Education and Ministry assists people who are preparing to enter special ministries as ordained deacons or elders and maintains standards and procedures for certification of people who plan to enter professional church-related ministries. This board gives general oversight and care to institutions of higher education, including schools, colleges, universities, and theological seminaries. This board recruits and provides general oversight for campus ministers and chaplains.

Commissions

The General Commission on Christian Unity and Interreligious Concerns works to accomplish a ministry and mission that reflects the oneness of Christ's church. It interprets the work, the issues, and relationships of The United Methodist Church to ecumenical and interreligious organizations and works to establish relationships with those of other faiths, cultures, and ideologies.

The General Commission on Religion and Race fosters a ministry of racial and ethnic participation in the work of the denomination. It works with the general agencies, institutions, and connectional structures to ensure racial and ethnic inclusiveness in the total life of the church.

The General Commission on United Methodist Men coordinates and provides resources for a ministry of spiritual growth and discipleship among men in the church.

The General Commission on the Status and Role of Women works toward the full and equal responsibility and participation of women in the total life and mission of the church, whereby they share fully in the power and policy making at all levels of the church's life.

Administrative Agencies

The United Methodist Church has four administrative agencies.

The General Board of Pension and Health Benefits is responsible for providing pension and benefit coverage for the laity and clergy (and their families) who have dedicated themselves to ministry in The United Methodist Church.

The United Methodist Publishing House publishes and distributes church school curriculum materials, books, and multimedia resources for the church.

The General Commission on Archives and History gathers, preserves, holds title to, and disseminates material on the history of The United Methodist Church and organizations that were its predecessors. This commission encourages and supports the work of annual conference and jurisdictional historical organizations. It is responsible for the policies related to designated United Methodist Historic Sites and United Methodist Heritage Landmarks.

The General Commission on Communication is the news-gathering and news-distributing agency for the church. It meets the communication, public-relations, and promotional needs of the entire church as it produces and distributes audiovisuals and is involved in television and other telecommunication ministries, such as cable, videocassette, CD, satellite, and other technologies that may become available. The commission provides answers to questions about the church and the church's ministry through Infoserv (phone: 800-251-8140 [toll free], or 615-742-5420; fax: 615-742-5423; e-mail: infoserv@umcom.umc.org; Internet: infoserv.umc.org).

World Service

Each congregation has the privilege of sharing in the church's evangelistic outreach, Christian nurture, servant ministries, and national and world mission work that is made possible by United Methodist boards and agencies through the World Service Fund. This apportioned fund supports the minimal needs for the mission and ministry of the church and is the first benevolent responsibility of the church.

Our Ecumenical Outreach

John Wesley said, "Would to God that all the party names, and unscriptural phrases and forms, which have divided the Christian world, were forgot; and that we might all agree to sit down together, as humble, loving disciples, at the feet of our common Master, to hear his word, to imbibe in his Spirit, and to transcribe his life in our own!"[3]

We are United Methodists, united with Christ and, in and through Christ, with all other brothers and sisters of the Christian faith. Ours is a long history of ecumenical cooperation. The United Methodist Church seeks opportunities to pray, study, and work together with Christians of other churches. The problems of needy people and a broken world demand the witness and united efforts of Christian churches working together. Our unity is in Christ. We are committed to our oneness in Christ. We are all part of the same body of Christ.

The United Methodist Church is a member not only of the World Methodist Council, formed in 1881, but also of the Consultation on Church Union (Churches Uniting in Christ), the National Council of Churches of Christ in the U.S.A., and the World Council of Churches. We work with other churches through these ecumenical organizations and interpret and evaluate the work of these groups in our own denomination.

We Thank God

Yes, we claim a rich heritage. We are indebted to those who have walked the path of faithfulness before us. We thank God for all that God has done through the years that has led to The United Methodist Church. We thank God that we have been brought to this hour. Called to witness and service, we greet the future with the assurance that nothing "will be able to separate us from the love of God in Christ Jesus our Lord" (Romans 8:39). God is with us. Thanks be to God!

ENDNOTES

CHAPTER 1: OUR JOURNEY OF FAITH

1. From "O For a Thousand Tongues to Sing," by Charles Wesley.
2. From "O For a Thousand Tongues to Sing," by Charles Wesley.
3. From *The Church,* by Hans Küng; pages 130–31. Reprinted by permission of Sheed and Ward, an apostolate of the Priests of the Sacred Heart, Franklin, WI. 2001.
4. From Sermon 1, "Salvation By Faith," by John Wesley.
5. From "The Lord's Prayer" (from The Ritual of the Former Methodist Church), in *The United Methodist Hymnal,* 895.
6. From "A New Creed," in *Voices United: The Hymn and Worship Book of The United Church of Canada;* page 918. The United Church Publishing House, 1996. Used by permission.

CHAPTER 2: UNITED IN CHRIST

1. From "A Service of Death and Resurrection" in *The United Methodist Book of Worship,* page 143. © 1979, 1980, 1985, 1989, 1992 The United Methodist Publishing House. Used by permission.
2. From *Jacob Albright and His Co-Laborers,* by R. Yeakel; page 35. © 1883 Publishing House of The Evangelical Association.
3. From Sermon 39, "Catholic Spirit," by John Wesley.
4. From "The Order for the Administration of the Sacrament of the Lord's Supper or Holy Communion," in *The Book of Hymns: Official Hymnal of The United Methodist Church,* 830. © 1964, 1966 Board of Publication of The Methodist Church, Inc. Used by permission of The United Methodist Publishing House.
5. From *The Confessions of Saint Augustine,* translated by Edward Bouverie Pusey. © 1909 Chatto & Windus.
6. From "Lord, I Want to Be a Christian," an Afro-American spiritual, in *The United Methodist Hymnal,* 402.
7. From "Foreign Missions in Battle Array," by Vachel Lindsay.
8. Adapted from *They Dared to Live,* by Robert M. Bartlett; pages 111–12. © 1937 The International Committee of Young Men's Christian Associations. Used by permission of Ayer Co. Publishers.

CHAPTER 3: OUR METHODIST ROOTS

1. From "Letters From the Reverend John Wesley to Various Persons."
2. From "Journal From October 14, 1735, to February 1, 1738," journal entry on February 7, 1736, by John Wesley.
3. From "Journal From February 1, 1738, to August 12, 1738," journal entry on March 4, 1738, by John Wesley.
4. From "The Journal of Charles Wesley: May 1, 1738, to August 31, 1738," journal entry on May 11, 1738, by Charles Wesley.
5. From "The Journal of Charles Wesley: May 1, 1738, to August 31, 1738," journal entry on May 21, 1738, by Charles Wesley.
6. From "The Journal of Charles Wesley: May 1, 1738, to August 31, 1738," journal entry on May 21, 1738, by Charles Wesley.
7. From "The Journal of Charles Wesley: May 1, 1738, to August 31, 1738," journal entry on May 23, 1738, by Charles Wesley.
8. From "Where Shall My Wondering Soul Begin," by Charles Wesley.
9. From "Journal From February 1, 1738, to August 12, 1738," journal entry on May 24, 1738, by John Wesley.
10. From "Journal From February 1, 1738, to August 12, 1738," journal entry on June 7, 1738, by John Wesley.
11. From "Journal From September 3, 1741, to October 27, 1743," journal entry on June 6, 1742, by John Wesley.
12. From "Journal From August 12, 1738, to November 1, 1739," journal entry on June 11, 1739, by John Wesley.
13. From "A Plain Account of Christian Perfection," by John Wesley.

CHAPTER 4: OUR UNITED BRETHREN ROOTS

1. From *The Life of Rev. Philip William Otterbein*, by Rev. A. W. Drury; page 47. © 1884 Rev. W. J. Shuey.
2. From *The Life of Rev. Philip William Otterbein*, by Rev. A. W. Drury; page 52. © 1884 Rev. W. J. Shuey.
3. From *The Life of Rev. Philip William Otterbein*, by Rev. A. W. Drury; page 53. © 1884 Rev. W. J. Shuey.
4. From *The Life of Rev. Philip William Otterbein*, by Rev. A. W. Drury; page 68. © 1884 Rev. W. J. Shuey.
5. From *The Life of Rev. Philip William Otterbein*, by Rev. A. W. Drury; page 103. © 1884 Rev. W. J. Shuey.
6. From *The Life of Rev. Philip William Otterbein*, by Rev. A. W. Drury; page 132. © 1884 Rev. W. J. Shuey.

7. From *The Life of Rev. Philip William Otterbein*, by Rev. A. W. Drury; page 365. © 1884 Rev. W. J. Shuey.

Chapter 5: Our Evangelical Roots

1. From *A History of The Evangelical Church*, by Raymond W. Albright; page 31. © 1942 The Evangelical Press. Used by permission of The United Methodist Publishing House.
2. From *A History of The Evangelical Church*, by Raymond W. Albright; page 34. © 1942 The Evangelical Press. Used by permission of The United Methodist Publishing House.
3. From *The History of The Evangelical United Brethren Church*, by J. Bruce Behney and Paul H. Eller; page 69. © 1979 Abingdon Press. Used by permission.
4. From *A History of The Evangelical Church*, by Raymond W. Albright; page 36. © 1942 The Evangelical Press. Used by permission of The United Methodist Publishing House.
5. From *The History of The Evangelical United Brethren Church*, by J. Bruce Behney and Paul H. Eller; page 84. © 1979 Abingdon Press. Used by permission.
6. From *A History of The Evangelical Church*, by Raymond W. Albright; page 91. © 1942 The Evangelical Press. Used by permission of The United Methodist Publishing House.

Chapter 6: Two Centuries of Ministry

1. From *Jacob Albright and His Co-Laborers*, by R. Yeakel; page 119. © 1883 Publishing House of The Evangelical Association.
2. From *Philip William Otterbein: Pastor/Ecumenist*, by Arthur C. Core; page 69. © 1968 The Board of Publication, The Evangelical United Brethren Church. Used by permission of The United Methodist Publishing House.
3. From "Methodism and Ecumenical Christianity," by Ivan Lee Holt, in *Methodism*, edited by William K. Anderson; page 283. © 1947 Stone and Pierce. Used by permission of The United Methodist Publishing House.
4. From Sermon 39, "Catholic Spirit," by John Wesley.
5. From *The Book of Discipline of The United Methodist Church—2004*; ¶ 5, page 23. Copyright © 2004 The United Methodist Publishing House. Used by permission.

6. From *The History of The Evangelical United Brethren Church,* by
   J. Bruce Behney and Paul H. Eller; page 392. © 1979 Abingdon
   Press. Used by permission.
7. From "Thoughts Upon Methodism," by John Wesley.

Chapter 7: What We Believe

1. From *The Book of Discipline of The United Methodist Church—2004;*
   ¶ 102, page 50. Copyright © 2004 The United Methodist Publishing
   House. Used by permission.
2. From *The Book of Discipline of The United Methodist Church—2004;*
   ¶ 102, page 51. Copyright © 2004 The United Methodist Publishing
   House. Used by permission.
3. From "O For a Faith That Will Not Shrink," words by William H.
   Bathurst (1796–1877).
4. From *The Book of Discipline of The United Methodist Church—2004;*
   ¶ 104, pages 76–77. Copyright © 2004 The United Methodist
   Publishing House. Used by permission.
5. From *The Book of Discipline of The United Methodist Church—2004;*
   ¶ 104, page 78. Copyright © 2004 The United Methodist Publishing
   House. Used by permission.
6. From *The Book of Discipline of The United Methodist Church—2004;*
   ¶ 104, page 81. Copyright © 2004 The United Methodist Publishing
   House. Used by permission.
7. From "The Nature, Design, and General Rules of the United
   Societies," by John Wesley.
8. From "The Church's One Foundation," words by Samuel J. Stone
   (1866).
9. From "The Lord's Prayer" (from The Ritual of the Former
   Methodist Church), in *The United Methodist Hymnal,* 895.
10. From *The Book of Discipline of The United Methodist Church—2004;*
    ¶ 101, page 46. Copyright © 2004 The United Methodist Publishing
    House. Used by permission.
11. From *The Book of Discipline of The United Methodist Church—2004;*
    ¶ 101, page 46. Copyright © 2004 The United Methodist Publishing
    House. Used by permission.
12. From *The Book of Discipline of The United Methodist Church—2004;*
    ¶ 214, page 134. Copyright © 2004 The United Methodist
    Publishing House. Used by permission.

13. From *The Book of Discipline of The United Methodist Church—2004;* ¶ 130, page 90. Copyright © 2004 The United Methodist Publishing House. Used by permission.
14. From *The Book of Discipline of The United Methodist Church—2004;* ¶ 103, page 63. Copyright © 2004 The United Methodist Publishing House. Used by permission.
15. From "A Service of Word and Table IV," in *The United Methodist Hymnal,* page 26. © 1957 Board of Publication, Evangelical United Brethren Church; © 1964, 1965, 1989 The United Methodist Publishing House. Used by permission.

CHAPTER 8: MEMBERSHIP IN THE UNITED METHODIST CHURCH

1. From "Baptismal Covenant II," in *The United Methodist Hymnal,* page 40. © 1976, 1980, 1985, 1989 The United Methodist Publishing House. Used by permission.
2. From "Baptismal Covenant II," in *The United Methodist Hymnal,* page 40. © 1976, 1980, 1985, 1989 The United Methodist Publishing House. Used by permission.
3. From "Baptismal Covenant I," in *The United Methodist Hymnal,* pages 33–34. © 1976, 1980, 1985, 1989 The United Methodist Publishing House. Used by permission.
4. From "Baptismal Covenant I," in *The United Methodist Hymnal,* page 37. © 1976, 1980, 1985, 1989 The United Methodist Publishing House. Used by permission.
5. From "Baptismal Covenant I," in *The United Methodist Hymnal,* page 38. © 1976, 1980, 1985, 1989 The United Methodist Publishing House. Used by permission.
6. From "Baptismal Covenant I," in *The United Methodist Hymnal,* page 38. © 1976, 1980, 1985, 1989 The United Methodist Publishing House. Used by permission.
7. From "The Lord's Prayer" (from The Ritual of the Former Methodist Church), in *The United Methodist Hymnal,* 895.
8. From "God of Grace and God of Glory," words by Harry Emerson Fosdick, in *The United Methodist Hymnal,* 577. Used by permission.
9. From "Prayer Is the Soul's Sincere Desire," by James Montgomery (1818).

CHAPTER 9: THE LAITY IN MINISTRY

1. From *The Book of Discipline of The United Methodist Church—2004;*
¶ 126, page 89. Copyright © 2004 The United Methodist Publishing House. Used by permission.
2. From "A Charge to Keep I Have," words by Charles Wesley (1762), in *The United Methodist Hymnal,* 413.
3. From "The Nature, Design, and General Rules of the United Societies," by John Wesley.
4. From *The Book of Discipline of The United Methodist Church—2004;*
¶ 126, page 89. Copyright © 2004 The United Methodist Publishing House. Used by permission.
5. From *The Book of Discipline of The United Methodist Church—2004;*
¶ 166, page 124. Copyright © 2004 The United Methodist Publishing House. Used by permission.
6. From "Minutes of Several Conversations Between the Rev. Mr. Wesley and Others, From the Year 1744, to the Year 1789," by John Wesley.
7. From *A Collection of Hymns for the Use of the People Called Methodists,* by John Wesley.
8. From *Evangelism and Theology in the Wesleyan Spirit,* by Albert C. Outler; page 39. © 1996 Discipleship Resources. Used by permission.

CHAPTER 10: THE CONGREGATION IN MISSION

1. From *The Book of Discipline of The United Methodist Church—2004;*
¶ 124, page 89. Copyright © 2004 The United Methodist Publishing House. Used by permission.
2. From *The Book of Discipline of The United Methodist Church—2004;*
¶ 201, page 127. Copyright © 2004 The United Methodist Publishing House. Used by permission.
3. From *The United Methodist Way,* by Branson L. Thurston; page 15. © 1983 Discipleship Resources. Used by permission.
4. From *Foundations: Shaping the Ministry of Christian Education in Your Congregation,* page 5. © 1993 Discipleship Resources. Used by permission.
5. From "O For a Closer Walk With God," words by William Cowper (1731–1800), in *The Book of Hymns: Official Hymnal of The United Methodist Church;* 268.
6. From prayers on plaques at the Coventry Cathedral of England.

CHAPTER 11: THE LOCAL CHURCH AND ITS CONNECTIONS

1. From *The Book of Discipline of The United Methodist Church—2004;* ¶ 305, page 198. Copyright © 2004 The United Methodist Publishing House. Used by permission.
2. From *The Book of Discipline of The United Methodist Church—2004;* ¶ 243, page 150. Copyright © 2004 The United Methodist Publishing House. Used by permission.
3. From "Explanatory Notes Upon the New Testament," by John Wesley.